Rights, Cultures, Subjects and Citizens

This book questions the political logic of foregrounding cultural collectives in a world shaped by globalization and neoliberalization. Throughout the world, it is no longer only individuals, but increasingly collective "cultures" who are made responsible for their own regulation, welfare and enterprise. This appears as a surprising shift from the tenets of classical liberalism which defined the ideal subject of politics as the "unencumbered self"- the free, equal and self-governing individual.

The increasing promotion and recognition of cultural rights in international legislation, multiculturalism, and public debates on "culture" as a political problem more generally indicate that culture has become a more central terrain for governance and struggles around rights and citizenship. On the basis of case studies from China, Latin America, and North America, the contributors of this book explore the links between culture, civility, and the politics of citizenship. They argue that official reifications of "culture" in relation to citizenship, and even the recognition of cultural rights, may obey strategies of governance and control, but that citizens may still use new cultural rights and networks, and the legal mechanisms that have been created to protect them, in order to pursue their own agendas of empowerment.

This book was originally published as a special issue of *Economy and Society*.

Susanne Brandtstädter is Professor of Social Anthropology at the University of Oslo, Norway. Her research in China has focussed on gender and social relatedness, moral economies, modernity and peasant subjectivities, legal knowledge, notions of justice, social and political rights, and local responses to global capitalism. Previous publications include *Chinese Kinship. New Anthropological Perspectives* (2009).

Peter Wade is Professor of Social Anthropology at the University of Manchester, UK. He works on race and ethnicity - and their articulations with gender - in Latin America and on ideas of race, nature and culture generally.

His recent work is on race and genomic science in Latin America. Previous publications include *Race and Sex in Latin America* (2009).

Kath Woodward is Professor of Sociology at the Open University, UK. She works on diversity, mobilities and inequalities, especially in relation to sex gender and embodied practices and the relationship between virtual and material forms of inequality, most recently in the field of sport. Previous publications include *Sex Power and the Games* (2012).

Rights, Cultures, Subjects and Citizens

Edited by
Susanne Brandtstädter, Peter Wade and Kath Woodward

Routledge
Taylor & Francis Group

LONDON AND NEW YORK

First published 2013
by Routledge
2 Park Square, Milton Park, Abingdon, Oxfordshire OX14 4RN

Simultaneously published in the USA and Canada
by Routledge
711 Third Avenue, New York, NY 10017

First issued in paperback 2015

Routledge is an imprint of the Taylor & Francis Group, an informa business

© 2013 Taylor & Francis

This book is a reproduction of *Economy and Society*, volume 40, issue 2. The Publisher requests to those authors who may be citing this book to state, also, the bibliographical details of the special issue on which the book was based.

British Library Cataloguing in Publication Data
A catalogue record for this book is available from the British Library

ISBN 13: 978-1-138-94564-7 (pbk)
ISBN 13: 978-0-415-63127-3 (hbk)

Typeset in Times New Roman
by Taylor & Francis Books

Publisher's Note
The publisher would like to make readers aware that the chapters in this book may be referred to as articles as they are identical to the articles published in the special issue. The publisher accepts responsibility for any inconsistencies that may have arisen in the course of preparing this volume for print.

Contents

Citation Information

The chapters in this book were originally published in the *Economy and Society,* volume 40, issue 2 (May 2011). When citing this material, please use the original page numbering for each article, as follows:

Chapter 6

Subjectification and Education for Quality in China
Andrew B. Kipnis
Economy and Society, volume 40, issue 2 (May 2011) pp. 289-306

Notes on Contributors

Charles R. Hale is Professor of Anthropology at the University of Texas, Austin, USA. Previous publications include *Resistance and contradiction: Miskitu Indians and the Nicaraguan state, 1894-1987* (1994), *Racismo en Guatemala: Abriendo debate sobre un tema tabú* (1999), *Memorias del mestizaje: Cultura y política en Centroamérica, 1920 al presente* (2004) and *'Ma's que un indio...': Racial ambivalence and neoliberal multiculturalism in Guatemala* (2006). He is also editor of the volume, *Engaging contradictions: Theory, politics and methods of activist scholarship* and author of numerous articles on identity politics, racism, neoliberalism and resistance among indigenous peoples of Latin America. He was President of the Latin American Studies Association from April 2006 through to October 2007 and began a four-year term as Director of the Teresa Lozano Long Institute of Latin American Studies in September 2009.

Nina Glick Schiller is a professor of social anthropology and the Director of the Research Institute for Cosmopolitan Cultures, University of Manchester, UK. Known for her work on transnational migration, particularly her 1994 book *Nations unbound: Transnational projects, postcolonial predicaments, and deterritorialized nation-states* (co-authored with L. Basch and C. Szanton Blanc), Glick Schiller's more recent work includes: *Georges woke up laughing: Long distance nationalism and the search for home* (2001), *Migration, development, and transnationalization: A critical stance* (2010), *Cosmopolitan sociability: Locating transnational religious and diasporic networks* (2011) and *Locating migration: Rescaling cities and migrants* (2011).

Andrew B. Kipnis is a Senior Fellow in Anthropology and Political and Social Change at the Australian National University, Australia. He is co-editor of *The China Journal* and author of *Governing educational desire: Culture, politics and schooling in China* (2011), *China and postsocialist anthropology: Theorizing power and society after communism* (2008), and *Producing guanxi: Sentiment, self and subculture in a North China village* (1997).

Rachel Sieder studied international relations, politics and Latin American Studies at the University of London, UK. She is currently Research Professor at the Centro de Investigaciones y Estudios Superiores en Antropología Social (CIESAS) in Mexico City, USA. She previously taught at the Institute for the Study of the Americas, University of London, UK, where she is now a research fellow. She is also an associate research professor at the Christian Michelsen Institute, University of Bergen, Norway. Her edited books include *Multiculturalism in Latin America: Indigenous rights, diversity and democracy* (2002), *The judicialization of politics in Latin America* (2005) and *Judicialization and political activism in Latin America* (2010). Her current research is on indigenous law and indigenous rights in Latin America.

Introduction: rights, cultures, subjects and citizens

Susanne Brandtstädter, Peter Wade and
Kath Woodward

This special issue arose from a concern with the political logic of the fore-grounding of collective culture(s) in the context of changing citizenship regimes.[1] Its key focus is the conjuncture in which 'culture' – claims of a collective distinction concerning heritage, location, moralities and values – has become the terrain of political struggles over the subject of rights in national and international politics, the re-allocation of entitlements, definitions of value and new forms of political representation. This appears to be linked to con-temporary processes of neoliberalization, the politics of which are often defined in terms of economic policies promoting private accumulation, entrepreneur-ship and free markets, but which typically also include a project of governance in which not only individuals, but also collective agents – which may be 'cultural' entities – are charged with increasing responsibility for their own regulation, welfare and enterprise, but in a depoliticized and bureaucratized mode (Santos, 2005). Citizenship is central here as the modern political and legal institution which links certain notions of personal rights and duties with the structures of governance and political agency, on the one hand, and with the national and, by extension, transnational economy, on the other.

Citizenship, as a sociological concept has been classified as involving political and legal, as well as cultural and social aspects that inform an individual's possibilities of participation in the public sphere (Marshall, 1964). In classic liberalism, the concept of citizenship linked ideas of merit or 'civilization' with that of the 'unencumbered self' (Sandel, 1984), evoking a unitary political subject whose rights were not just derived from the state or other law-making institutions, but extrapolated from self-owned 'freedoms', that is, from human self-actualization as a self-governing, economizing and self-sustained individual. There is a clear tension between the historically specific classic liberal perspective on human nature, individual equality and citizenship and current trends within a global 'neoliberal' context towards state recognition of cultural difference and identity as the basis for new forms of citizen rights, now broadly understood to include not only political but also cultural rights. This active recognition has been linked to the success of grassroots movements ranging from the civil rights struggles of the 1960s, to de-colonialization movements, anti-racist movements, indigenous movements and gay/lesbian movements – the so-called 'new social movements' – which highlighted the potential ethnocentric, sexist, class-based and racist assumptions said by critics to underlie the categories and practices of citizenship. These struggles, to a large extent, went beyond claiming formal political citizenship or the right to vote (which struggles had already widely achieved, although, for women, not until well into the twentieth century), and pushed instead for integrative forms of cultural and social citizenship and the legalizing of practices central to this. This resulted in a progressive reformulation of legislations to allow more room for cultural diversity, acceptance of the value of different historical experiences, ways of living and of cultural expression, and the protection of diverse cultural heritage, if necessary through legislating particular and collective cultural rights (as in the case of indigenous peoples in Latin America and elsewhere).

Increasingly, however, the narrative of a grassroots victory defining this process of integration through difference is being challenged by theoretical perspectives which point out that the reification of cultures as a source of shared values, internal discipline and differentiation against various others might not, especially in a *neoliberal* context, necessarily clash with an interest in producing self-governing (i.e. disciplined and thus 'free') citizens, or with the aim of governments to control and regulate populations, or with goals of class restoration, capital accumulation and oligarchic rule (Harvey, 2005; Žižek, 1997). Nikolas Rose (1999, ch. 5), for example, argues that culture has emerged as a 'third space' of governing, allowing 'advanced liberalism' to combine a rolling back of the state and an expansion of market principles with new forms of disciplining citizens and controlling social anomie. For Rose, not only is collective culture thus *not* opposed to liberalism in an 'advanced' stage, but, as part of an overall process of privatization, new cultural communities become the extended arm of governments intent on 'outsourcing' public functions; in this sense, a reconstituted 'culture' becomes one arena to produce 'free' citizens.

We might add here that these developments – which even made inroads into the People's Republic of China as part of a government strategy to secure party control and successfully compete on the global market (Zhang & Ong, 2008) – obviously have some relation to the collapse of an older 'socialist alternative' whose oppositional presence shaped liberal government in the decades before. The Cold War opposition between individualism and collectivism, which sustained governing discourses and forms of citizenship on both sides (Brandtstädter, 2007), appears to have collapsed into a new global 'harmony' of governance involving a pervasive anti-politics discourse, a celebration of markets and law as rational, as well as 'just', mechanisms of social regulation, a new acceptance of political authoritarianism and surveillance (despite a discourse of widening choice and citizen participation) and a 'culture agenda' that appears to be the object of incessant public debates, obsessions and anxieties.

This 'culture agenda' appears as the distinguishing moment between classic liberal visions of a civil society, made up of 'unencumbered selves' organized on the basis of individual interest and choice, and a neoliberal acceptance of culture as a source of identity politics, different 'types' of subjects and forms of social organization. A multicultural turn is certainly most striking in classic liberal countries like the UK and the US, but also Latin America where the notion of citizenship followed the original liberal model, but where too new forms of cultural expression by 'marked others' (as against the un-marked citizen) have gained more presence in the public sphere, and where especially indigenous people have achieved important legal protection. Writing from the Latin American experience, Charles Hale suggests that 'compensatory measures to disadvantaged cultural groups . . . are an integral part of neoliberal ideology. These distinctive cultural politics (along with their socio-political counterparts), rather than simply the temporal lapse between classic liberalism and its latter day incarnation, are what give the "neo" its real meaning' (2005, p. 12).

Yet, we believe that to understand the use of 'culture' and cultural difference in contemporary politics and processes of governance, it is important to recognize the depth of history and a geographical spread that nuances a presumed link between neoliberalism and multiculturalism. After all, colonial policies in the British Empire enshrined cultural differences in ways that paralleled later mechanisms of governance in apartheid South Africa. Moreover, as the papers in this special issue show, the 'culture agenda' is not confined to societies run on liberal principles. As a radical modern ideology, socialism, like liberalism, was theoretically hostile to pre-modern cultural formations. Nevertheless, socialist empires (such as the Soviet Union and the People's Republic of China) reified minority cultures by applying the Stalinist definition of ethnos to classify separate ethnic groups, and often implemented 'autonomous territories' in traditional settlement areas. Minority cultures – and even 'peasant culture' in China (Cohen, 2005, ch. 3) – were clearly reconstituted in the interest of socialist development and centralized party control. Ethnic customs and traditions were supported when they 'coloured' the vision of socialist internationalism within one state (see Kandiyoti, 2000) and did not obstruct state-making. If they appeared politically 'harmful' or – to use a Chinese term – 'splittist', then they were (and still are) violently repressed. Socialist cultural politics are not the same as liberal multiculturalism, but they nevertheless demonstrate striking parallels to multiculturalism as a mode of making 'others' and of governing diversity within one state. Such 'harmonies' have become very evident in the case of contemporary China. Here, where the issue of culture – both minority and Han – became a topic of obsessive public debates in the 1980s (see Wang, 1996, ch. 2), the government promotes 'good' cultural traditions that support overall 'societal harmony', while expressive 'local' culture is being rapidly commodified for tourist consumption and has become an important source of government revenue. At the same time, custom-culture and 'civilizedness' – the latter defined as characterizing the ideal citizen subject – stand in a contradictory relation, which constantly produces internal cultural others that help to (re)define civilization 'with Chinese characteristics'. As Asad says: 'The claim that many radical critics make that hegemonic power necessarily suppresses difference in favour of unity is quite mistaken. Just as mistaken is their claim that power always abhors ambiguity. To secure its unity – to make its own history – dominant power has worked best through differentiating and classifying practices' (1993, p. 17).

Still, the increasing promotion and recognition of cultural rights in international legislation and the spread of official multiculturalism in many areas of the world, as well as the proliferation of public debates on 'culture' as political problem more generally, indicate that it has arguably become an ever more central terrain for governance and struggles around rights and citizenship, especially as the object of judicial or quasi-judicial legislation. Of course, the politics of culture are realized within the framework of different states, giving them a different spin and historical trajectory in each case. As the papers in this issue demonstrate, they must be analysed with ethnographic sensitivity to these specific local and national dynamics. Nevertheless, by combining case studies from different world regions, we hope that a cross-cultural comparison sheds more light on the political dynamics of regulation and democratic empowerment through 'culture'.

The following papers take up various strands of these issues and lines of argument, in order to re-examine the particular conjuncture between opportunities for political and legal action, the affirmation of collective cultures, globalization and government regulation. All the papers, from various perspectives, explore the relation between culture (as collective values), civility (as the formation moral and social subjectivities) and the politics of citizenship. But, instead of assuming a hidden systemic logic which, when discovered, would resolve the tension between cultural difference and citizenship in one or the other way, we insist on the importance of an ethnographic exploration of particular cases and on a comparative approach to understanding processes of political subject becoming and regulation in new citizenship regimes. That is, we do not accept that opposites are being collapsed into one another (along the lines of 'war is peace'), but insist on the tensions between democracy and inequality, equality and hierarchy, sameness and uniqueness, liberty and order, freedom and coercion. A key thread linking the papers is the idea that official reifications of 'culture' as part of the package of citizenship, and even the recognition of cultural rights, may obey state strategies of governance and control (often, but not always, linked to neoliberal agendas), but that, at the same time, citizens may use new cultural rights and networks, and the legal mechanisms that have been created to protect them, in order to pursue their own agendas of empowerment.

Liberalism and its contradictions

Liberalism is not the main political rationality underlying all the contexts examined here – China being an obvious exception. But it has been central to the USA (Glick Schiller's geographical focus) and Latin America (Hale's and Sieder's focus). In addition, it has been suggested that in China a 'new social' is organized along economic and legal principles that respond not just to the party state but also to the forces of neoliberal globalization, and that this has emerged as the source of new subjectivities, and strategies of self-regulation and of citizen-becoming (Zhang & Ong, 2008; see also Fong & Murphy, 2006). Most importantly, all the countries examined by the authors in this special issue are influenced by an international context shaped powerfully by liberal principles of economic practice as well as notions of (cultural) citizen-ship rights that emerge from a liberal political rationality and the contra-dictions and tensions underlying it. In view of this, it is useful to examine briefly the liberal notions of citizenship and political order that have shaped Western European and American contexts.

In the Americas, indigenous populations and the import of African slaves made the original liberal question 'who can rule' (Rose & Miller, 2008, p. 206) the basis for new diversified forms of citizenship and of strategies of inclusion and exclusion centring on the 'problem' of 'racial' (and also cultural) others. Also in Western Europe, the formation of liberalism, as well as its political 'protoform' secular enlightenment, is historically related to the experience of religious wars and colonial encounters with 'savages' living beyond the borders of the 'civilized' world, which have had a profound influence on ideas of the rational, free citizen (Asad, 2003). The political theory of liberalism, with its emphasis on natural rights as the foundation of citizen rights, implies a sharing of at least similar views of what rights and duties involve, in short, it means the sharing of a worldview – which liberalism might call civilization, but which itself can be described as a particular cultural form or mode, articulated with a national one. Classic liberalism, promoting freedom and equal rights, was from the beginning deeply invested in cultural hierarchization, exposing an ideology best characterized with the old joke that 'all are equal but some are more equal than others'. For John Locke, it was the possession of reason that led to acceptance of the law, while emotional temperance – a quality exemplified by male, property-owning Englishmen – was the condition for self-government. Others, such as women, wage labourers, children and servants, who did not fully possess such temperance and lacked the proper education had to be excluded from political society (Mehta, 1997, pp. 65–70). Early British political liberalism, as well as French, excluded large swathes of the population from the right to vote, as John Stuart Mill argued in *The subjection of women*

(1929 [1869]). Mill answered the question 'who can rule' by drawing the line between civilization and barbarism. Civilization was the precondition for political citizenship as the epitome of universal human development. But it also had a concrete place and culture, which was that of Europe in general and Great Britain in particular. As he wrote in *On liberty*, for the uncivilized 'despotism is a legitimate mode of government ... *provided the end be their improvement*' (1975 [1859], pp. 15–16, quoted in Passavant, 1996, p. 312). In 'Considerations of representative government', he phrased the relation between liberal democracy and culture as one structured by authoritarianism – the 'first lesson of civilization [is] that of obedience' (1975 [1859], p. 202, in Passavant, 1996, p. 310).

This Millian paradigm, within a Europe reflected in deeply authoritarian family relations, was political practice in a colonial context. It can also easily be applied to modern China, where the aim of early twentieth-century modernizers to transform the population into a powerful nation resulted in the political rejection of its culturally 'backward' elements, and where, post-Mao, a political discourse on civilization and the rule of law has developed within a deeply authoritarian political environment (not to mention an exceedingly successful market economy). If the tension between universal equality and particular difference is the first tension within liberal ideology, then the tension between universal freedom and authoritarian discipline, or even total exclusion from 'civilized society', is the second. The third contradiction derives from the relation between freedom and equality, in so far as the idea of freedom presupposes human equality but leads to inequality, and hence to unfreedom. This is of course the contradiction where socialism intervened, replacing the liberal individual with the class subject, and the free market economy and private property with a planned state economy and public, or collective, property as the basis for socialist citizenship. Liberals may claim that liberalism only ever mandates equality of opportunity, but persistent inequality of outcome inevitably suggests that opportunities are not, in fact, equal, and only some of this inequality can be explained by different natural abilities. In fact, pursuing the opportunities open to one as an individual can lead to a structural hierarchy of unequal outcomes, which itself constrains equality of opportunity at a collective level. Further, if liberalism mandates that each individual has the right to autonomy and self-determination, then everyone is the same in this respect. But it is a short step from ideas of personal autonomy to ideas of personal identity and the desire that one's selfhood be recognized by others – which implies differentiation and distinction (Taylor & Gutmann, 1994, p. 43). This might be called a Romantic gloss on Enlightenment liberalism – a concern with the particular character or spirit of persons, nations, places – but it is also a tension that exists within classic liberalism itself. The autonomy of the self can be realized only when others recognize you as distinct and thus different. The autonomy that all individuals desire, and that liberalism vindicates as the key value which we (ideally) share equally, is paradoxically a dependent condition that depends on differentiation.

Citizenship and pluralism

Citizenship takes diverse and sometimes contradictory forms. Liberal thought presents particular sets of ideas about how citizenship can be configured and the benefits and responsibilities which wider participation in its regimes have to offer. Liberal regimes have used the politics of citizenship to deal with their own internal tensions and contradictions. The most common practice has been to exclude a subset of the population from political rights and the rights and freedoms enshrined in liberal citizenship, usually by virtue of a supposed incapacity to exercise such rights or discharge of the accompanying obligations. In this way, women, children, those without literary skills and those classified as racially other have all, in different places and at different times, been formally or informally excluded from public and political participation. In nineteenth-century Latin America, for example, many of the new states started with property-based requirements for suffrage and virtually all adopted literacy-based requirements later on, with some countries retaining such restrictions into the late twentieth century (e.g. Brazil until 1988 or Peru until 1979). In contrast, the USA moved from economic restrictions towards race-based requirements (until 1870, when this was outlawed) and thence to literacy requirements, until these were outlawed in 1965 (Engerman & Sokoloff, 2005). Literacy requirements notoriously discriminated against the poor and the non-white. As mentioned above, in the UK voting restrictions were based mainly on property and were successively loosened over the nineteenth century but not lifted until 1918. The first French Constitution (1791) made the distinction between active and passive citizens, with the latter being denied political rights. Gender remained an explicit bar to voting rights well into the twentieth century. Such formal *restrictions* were often justified by naturalizing ideologies, based on contemporary science that defined those excluded as less able to cope with the demands and privileges of full citizenship.

Classical liberalism is generally depicted as being 'culture-blind', as starting from the assumption of the 'unencumbered self' as the natural human. But, as we argued above, culture was always part of liberal citizen regimes in the negative: the coloured, the indigenous, the poor, the women were at various times and places seen as having a culture (often defined as irrational and passion-driven) incompatible with civilized citizenship (see Mehta, 1997). Also in a positive way liberalism was deeply entrenched with 'cultural pluralism', an entrenchment directly evident in the interchangeability of the terms 'citizen' and 'national'. The constitution of distinct national cultures appeared paramount here. In the United States, Indians were obviously 'natives', so *ius solis* should have applied. They were nevertheless excluded from citizenship for a long time: first, they were defined as 'incapacitated, by their mental debasement' and politically turned into wards of the state. Education as a way to citizen-becoming (Mills' suggestion) was then precluded by a second clause, which declared tribal Indians 'aliens' as they 'were born under the jurisdiction of their tribes and tribes [were] considered nations of some sovereignty within the territorial United States' (Holston, 2008, p. 54). In France it was 'the Jewish question' that was the issue for many debates over the relation between culture (combining religion and morality) and citizenship. Whereas those opposing Jewish citizenship argued that Jewish character and culture precluded their becoming French citizens, those in favour did not so much question the cultural argument, but maintained that French sovereignty could not allow Jews to become a separate nation within the nation; instead, they had to be granted citizenship *on an individual basis* (Holston, 2008, p. 44–5). In Latin America, nation-building in the nineteenth and early twentieth century was often based on ideas of *mestizaje* (racial and cultural mixture) which was said to produce a homogeneous, whitened citizen; in this blackness and indigenousness were generally seen as backward, primitive elements. Yet many Latin American elites were also cognizant, and sometimes appreciative, of the cultural diversity in their nations: a liberal tolerance was evident in some cases, as long as the basic direction of the nation's future was decided by elite white men (Wade, 2005).

Cultural difference and the governing of the social

Rose and Miller (2008, pp. 86–90) argue that by the early twentieth century governments in North America and Europe recognized that 'the social' was a domain for which they had to take some political responsibility, though they did so to a lesser extent than socialist governments did. It was now up to the state to intervene in protection, rights and justice and social solidarity for its citizen. This shift was not just confined to individual states, but also the basis of a transnational liberal order enshrined in international conventions such as the ILO's conventions on Indigenous and Tribal Peoples (Convention 107 of 1957 and the better known Convention 169 of 1989). By the mid to late twentieth century, such a concern had expanded to encompass the beginnings of state intervention in cultural difference and its consequences for equal opportunity. With this shift towards a greater recognition of difference, a distinction between identity (as a sense of being in relation to others) and citizenship (as a sense of being a citizen of the nation-state) has become increasingly blurred as the concept of citizenship extends into 'cultural' realms, strongly mediated by ideas of difference (Cowan *et al.*, 2001; Ong, 1999; Rosaldo, 1999; Wade, 2000; Wilson, 1996; Yuval-Davis & Werbner, 1999). Difference presents particular dilemmas for liberal conceptualizations of citizenship, which have been expressed in terms of the troubling tension between difference and equality within the cultural terrain (Woodward, 2009).

In the 1960s, the USA introduced affirmative action policies for its black citizens, Canada adopted multicultural politics in 1971 first in the interest of the French-speaking minority and later for its indigenous peoples. In the 1990s, a large number of Latin American states adopted constitutional and other legislative reforms to recognize, and in some cases give special rights to, ethnic minorities (Van Cott, 2000). Increased attention to diversity has not been limited to ethnic difference: gender difference remains a major driver of this trend, as is sexual difference and, to a lesser extent, age. Difference is, one could say, itself diversifying, by a mutually reinforcing demand for equal recognition for an increasing number of 'identities', and governing policies that seek to define, with an ever-expanding set of criteria, 'others' within national society. The causes of this overall shift are manifold: linked to international or, now, transnational movements for liberation and equal recognition, which often sought to introduce socialist elements into liberal society, and to new forms of international legislation couched in the language of human and cultural rights to enforce the recognition and protection of difference in national law (Latin America and Eastern Europe are cases in point). One result of this process has been the emergence of a kaleidoscope of standardized differences, which all reflect the nominal position of the 'normal citizen'; in other words, reflect on the particular national configuration of 'normalcy' (rather than dismantling it). This is also evident in government policy circles which assimilate all these axes of difference to 'diversity' in a commitment to social inclusivity or, in contemporary China, to 'social stability' and 'harmony'. Reform China does not formally recognize culture as the source of different types of legal citizenship or citizen rights. Nevertheless, variations on 'affirmative action' can be found in exemptions from the one-child policy for national minorities (and its less strict version for 'peasants'), and in local government investments' into regional cultural traditions and products deemed valuable from a historical, economic and national perspective. Representations of inclusion are sought after also in other arenas. For example, sport and leisure activities have increasingly become the target of social inclusion politics, implemented by a whole range of different apparatuses of voluntary as well as state organizations in Western countries like the USA or the UK (Woodward, 2007). Multicultural nation-building in Britain has even transformed 'traditional' forms of difference, such as class. Gillian Evans, for example, notes how working-class white Londoners are beginning to talk about their class position in cultural terms, in order to participate and be recognized as much as other 'ethnics'.[2]

Critics of multiculturalism have contended that liberalism is able to take account of difference and that the apparent contradiction between sameness/equality and difference/inequality is not politically paralysing insofar as a liberal rule of law allows a democratic openness in which the 'self-understanding of a collectivity' can make itself felt (Habermas, 2000, p. 217). Other common critiques make a different political point: namely, that multiculturalism creates divisions in society (along racial, ethnic, gender lines), that it ghettoizes cultural minorities and indeed limits the rights of their members (Bissoondath, 1994) and, above all, that it diverts attention from the underlying structural issue of class inequalities (Barry, 2000). Charles Hale (2002, 2005), in contrast, has proposed a more elaborate interrelation by coining the term 'neoliberal multiculturalism'. He argues that, while neoliberal market reforms and associated changes in governance seem to favour the individual as an autonomous actor in the market place, in fact neoliberalism is not as resistant to group rights and the idea of collective difference as its liberal tag leads one to expect. This is not so much because, as Habermas might contend, liberal democracies are able to deal with collective differences through the normal mechanisms of democracy and dialogue, but because it suits the purposes of government to institutionalize certain ethno-cultural categories and groups (thereby undermining the formation of others, of political *excess*), and to co-opt communities in *policing* this difference. In short, then, the 'culture agenda' may act as a mode of governance to control the effects of population diversity in a context of new transnational involvements, such as the international legal regimes discussed by Sieder in this special issue, which recognize certain entitlements on the basis of cultural difference. This may help explain why many states – and not just ones traditionally founded on liberal principles – have actively adopted a discourse on 'culture' (and cultural variety) not just to discriminate against various 'others', but as a growing 'third space' (Rose 1999) in which to regulate citizenship.

However, such a mode of governance can also supply 'communities' with new tools for self-understanding and political action, which may go against the intentions of the oligarchic state and other entities involved in decentralized modes of 'culturalist' governance. The papers in this special issue focus precisely on these dialectics of culture and citizen formation in diverse settings. We foreground contradictions, paradoxes and tensions to enquire into dynamics of control and emancipation, the reach of neoliberal policies over the formation of subjectivities, and into the relation between citizen rights, cultural diversity and transnational linkages.

Rights, cultures and (im)possible subjects: the papers

Charles Hale's paper outlines the key traits of what he has called neoliberal multiculturalism, with which many of the other papers engage, either explicitly or by introducing important nuances and/or comparative contexts. Hale explores the contradictions and entanglements of black and indigenous land rights struggles in Central America, focusing on a number of activist associations and their experiences. He demonstrates how contradictions between activists' goals and forms of accommodations, as well as problems involving political leadership and economic sustainability in territories which have gained some autonomy from the central state, are exacerbated by strategies of neoliberal governance and the emerging 'entrepreneurial' state. Paradoxically, he suggests, among the most daunting obstacles to liberatory action is not the repression or denial of rights, but, rather, partial recognition and the bureaucratic-political entanglements that follow in new regimes of 'neoliberal multiculturalism'. Collective territorial rights for indigenous groups have been justified on the basis of radical cultural difference, a view also recently adopted by institutions such as the World Bank, and increasingly accepted by Central

American states themselves. While collective cultural rights over territory seem to contradict both the interests of capitalist expansion and of the territorial state, Hale argues that they no longer do so, as these states, their modes of governance and their articulation with global capitalism have changed. Collective territorial rights for indigenous and black communities are granted in the context of the decreasing profitability of agriculture, and in economically marginal areas, for which a new entrepreneurial state withdraws responsibility, while allowing even more unfettered economic exploitation in other areas and, by fixing marginal communities in 'place', ensuring oligarchic rule. Nevertheless, a collective identification with a particular cultural heritage continues to provide the basis for grassroots mobilization and for utopian political projects. Hale suggests that a key to maintaining a radical critique of neoliberal hegemony is to re-link the 'pragmatic' struggle for economic resources with the politics of the 'impossible subject', a link that brought forth indigenous activism in the first place, but that neoliberal accommodations are increasingly successful in severing.

The paper by Nina Glick Schiller deals with the transnational foundations of contemporary nation-states and practices of citizenship, as well as the strategic denial of such foundations on the side of national policy-makers. Here, one effect of the liberal politics of naturalizing both equality and difference – namely the de-politicization of inequality – is discussed within a current, Western context of immigration, nationalism and multiculturalism. A political rhetoric on multiculture and value integration is contrasted with the situated social practices of activists and immigrants that create new forms of conviviality within neoliberalizing states.

Glick Schiller's paper examines the discourse on citizenship and cultural values in an immigrant-receiving city in the USA. She critiques the standard approach to immigration and citizenship that foregrounds the ethnic ties that migrants maintain to communities of origin. Instead she explores the religious affiliations that link migrants to potentially global networks. The city officials of Manchester, in New Hampshire, USA, deploy multiculturalism in an attempt to re-brand and promote their city in the face of its marginal status in the neoliberalizing USA. But migrants often avoided participating in or backing this multicultural agenda, at least in public displays (even if in more private, domestic settings, ethnic ties had continuing relevance in some respects). They instead preferred to engage in other fields of social connection, for example those generated by global religions (Buddhism, Islam and fundamentalist Christianity). The values espoused by these religions – rather conservative views of the family and sexuality, for example – tended to resonate rather well with those of New Hampshire natives. Migrant preferences for religious activity did not, however, correspond to a rejection of the city's attempts at neoliberal reform: at the level of family – rather than ethnic community – migrants were often eager to invest their time and resources in urban gentrification, city-centre regeneration and small business enterprise, using kin networks to underwrite such activities. Glick Schiller's article suggests that multiculturalism can be seen as a resource for neoliberal reformers – a de-politicized brand image – but that the actual operation of 'ethnic cultures' is more complex: migrants seek to challenge the economic inequality they face and work across public/private divides, using a variety of resources and networks – including religious and ethnic-kinship ones – to achieve this.

Glick Schiller examines neoliberal citizenship by focusing on forms of social inclusion that are not primarily ethnic or national, that are rooted in collective engagements and that can be contrasted with a discourse of national exclusiveness, cultural values, persistent inequalities and upward financial flows. Neoliberal agendas are linked to the commodification and marketing of (ethnic) culture as part of a policy of city governance and income generation. But migrants have an ambivalent response: they participate in urban regeneration in ways that, while they may support city policies, are aimed at consolidating family fortunes, not ethnic communities; at the same time, they reach beyond the multicultural agenda towards global religions. This nuances links between neoliberalism and multiculturalism. Not only can the subjects defined by multicultural policies use those policies to their advantage – as has often been observed – they can also engage resources that reach outside the scope of narrow multiculturalism.

The following papers by Sieder and Brandtstädter focus on how a judicialization of the political – a phenomenon that can be observed worldwide (e.g. Comaroff & Comaroff, 2006) – can lead to new exchanges between cultural politics, strategies of political participation through claims on 'rights' and the political economy. Sieder's paper is concerned with the politics of indigenous rights and multiculturalism in neoliberal Latin America and is the closest cousin to Hale's paper. Brandtstädter's paper speaks to these concerns from the 'reverse' perspective of 'neosocialist' China, where a new politics of creating self-regulating (rather than self-governing) citizens from the old socialist 'masses' has resulted in efforts to 're-culturalize' the peasant category as the nation's 'other'; a politics that is also contested by the new rural law activism. As in Hale's paper, land struggles form a key in peasants' efforts to turn such otherness into a source of emancipatory politics.

Rachel Sieder's paper focuses on the effects of the judicialization of the political struggle for indigenous rights in Guatemala. The context is one in which globalization and neoliberal reforms have increasingly de-linked law and the state, creating new forms of legal pluralism (e.g. international, national and 'local' law), new, non-judicial forms of dispute resolution, as well as fragmented patterns of legality. The judicialization of indigenous claims, as she points out, has sometimes led to cooptation and demobilization, and tends to fix ethnic categories by projecting an 'essentialized, idealised and atemporal indigenous identity'. Yet Sieder argues that the mere plurality of new legal forms, and especially the access to international legal norms and regulations, has also opened up opportunities for indigenous social movements to engage in 'counter-hegemonic' forms of law-making that can challenge dominant interests within state and industry. Sieder emphasizes the unpredictability, instability and often cumulative effects of collective action, in this case regarding the formulation of legal frameworks that reflect alternative perspectives on the fundamental concepts of property, the person, community and choice. The transnational dimension again emerges as especially relevant here, giving indigenous activists the possibility of expanding the space for, and thereby the scope of, political action. Sieder notes the emergence of guidelines adopted by major international funding agencies, such as the World Bank and the Inter-American Development Bank, which seek to protect the interests of indigenous (and increasingly Afro-Latin) peoples. While these are 'soft' norms, not legally enforceable and of questionable status in terms of their impact on actual lending policy and project development, they nevertheless open avenues for claims and redress. Of interest here is the way 'law', broadly conceived, expands beyond the scope of the state: this develops an important dimension in ideas about how neoliberalism links to multiculturalism and the promotion of cultural rights more widely.

Susanne Brandtstädter's paper focuses on struggles over the nature of peasants' citizenship in contemporary China, here a Maoist administrative category created in conjunction with that of urbanites. Reform China instituted limited forms of 'grassroots' democracy, allowed peasants already in the late 1970s to engage in entrepreneurial activities, and touted 'governing through law' and 'citizen rights' as a clear break with the Maoist era of movement politics. At the same time, as Brandtstädter argues, neosocialism sought to cut off peasants from the political by re-culturalizing the peasant category as the modern nation's negative other, a politics that found its concrete expression in land grabs and the 'fate' of many so-called 'peasant-workers' as exploited, culturally despised and semi-legalized 'immigrants' in China's cities. Focusing on the activities of rural rights defenders, Brandtstädter shows how these engage with the new discourse on law, civilization and citizenship in order to reject new exclusions and reclaim a collective political voice. What prevents their cooptation, also in the eyes of fellow peasants, is that they actively embrace 'peasantness' through maintaining their rural residence and bonding with other peasants, and by demonstrating political sincerity in 'living simple' (*pusu*), a Maoist term that turned (certain) aspects of peasant culture into a general citizen ideal and a radical critique of political corruption and the waste of public resources. Cultural fixation, on the other hand, is undermined by the valued citizen knowledge that formally 'uneducated' peasants demonstrate by skilfully engaging the law and often winning cases against local governments in rural courts. Brandtstädter argues that culture becomes a ground for new forms of political mobilization in so far as it gives rise to grassroots collective action, solidarity and a shared experience of political exclusion. On the other hand, it is precisely the appropriation of a (historically particular) 'universalist' citizen idiom as the language of law and rights, and practices that create links beyond 'traditional' boundaries of place and class – such as with journalists, academics, 'real' lawyers – that challenge the cultural order of the authoritarian state and create space for transformative political action. Brandtstädter's paper indicates that the consolidation of 'culture' – in her case, phrased in non-ethnic terms – and its use as both a mechanism of governance and a ground for resistance and transformation are not confined to contexts in which neoliberalism (and even less classic liberalism) are *prima facie* the dominant political-economic rationalities. Instead, the promotion of 'culture' clearly serves the purposes of a variety of modes of governance.

While Hale's and Brandtstädter's papers foreground the importance of, in Charles Hale's terms, the 'impossible subject' as a place from which to launch a political and cultural critique of hegemonic states, the special issue concludes with a paper by Andrew Kipnis that focuses on the process of subjectification itself, central to all theories of governance and political action. Exploring the case of 'education for quality' in China, he questions the often too taken-for-granted assumption of a direct 'fit' between 'processes of subjectification that are articulated by governance agents and the types of subjects that are actually produced' within particular social contexts. This assumption is particularly evident among those who explore 'neoliberal governmentality' and posit the emergence of a homogeneous neoliberal subject. In the case of Reform China, he shows that, under the slogan 'education for quality', educational strategies which aim to support the formation of a 'freer', creative and self-determined student subject sit uneasily with authoritarian discourses that demand subjection to a draconian examination regime as well as to the authority and 'truth' of the Party. These, in his view, cannot be reconciled, and do not provide a single coherent model of a citizen subject. 'Education for quality' is directly linked to the developmental aims of the reform state, and thus imbued by governing agents with a larger national agenda; *vice versa*, excelling in school or university is 'sold' in the dominant discourse as a form of patriotism asked of Chinese students. But Kipnis did not find much successful mobilization for 'hard work' among Chinese students for reasons of national development or patriotism. Rather the 'structured social relations' that most students were involved in at home and at school played a far greater role in the forming of student subjectivities. Relations with parents, for example, demanded studying hard as an expression of filial piety. Here again, governmental intentions to regulate subjectivities in favour of a particular national cultural project – the quality citizen, who does not challenge party hegemony – are undercut by the exchanges, relations and practices that make up the *social* person and form particular identities. Rather like Glick Schiller, Kipnis shows that people orient their goals towards family priorities, albeit the activities they pursue – business enterprises in the US, hard work in China – end up fitting in with agendas that are either neoliberal in the US case or projects to create self-regulating subjects in the case of China. Like Brandtstädter, Kipnis indicates that these orientations can be the source of resistance against top-down processes of subjectification and ideological hierarchies (a 'fact' that all socialist states, united in their mistrust of the 'private' and the 'domestic', knew). This again nuances the links that exist between neoliberalism and the deployment of reified notions of collective culture. This special issue thus ends at the other end of the (neoliberal) spectrum, the human individual. We conclude that cracks in existing hegemonies and alternative possibilities emerge through social engagement as a member of (and for) a particular collective – not an abstract 'cultural community', but a community of meaning, praxis and emotional attachment.

Notes

1   The papers in this special issue arose out of a workshop held at the University of Manchester on 26–7 March 2007 (except for the paper by Andrew Kipnis, which was a later addition). The workshop was organized by Susanne Brandtstädter, Peter Wade and Kath Woodward. It was funded by the ESRC Centre for Research into Socio-Cultural Change (CRESC), based at the University of Manchester and the Open University (see http://www.cresc.ac.uk/). It was held under the aegis of CRESC's Theme 3, which focused on 'Culture, Governance and Citizenship: The Formation and Transformations of Liberal Government', coordinated by Professor Tony Bennett, Open University.
2   This is the subject of an ongoing research project by Gillian Evans. See http://www.socialsciences.manchester.ac.uk/disciplines/socialanthropology/about/staff/evans/

References

Asad, T. (1993). *Genealogies of religion: Discipline and reasons of power in Christianity and Islam.* Baltimore, MD: Johns Hopkins University Press.

Asad, T. (2003). *Formations of the secular: Christianity, Islam, modernity.* Stanford, CA: Stanford University Press.

Barry, B. (2000). *Culture and equality: An egalitarian critique of multiculturalism.* Cambridge: Polity Press.

Bissoondath, N. (1994). *Selling illusions: The cult of multiculturalism in Canada.* Toronto: Penguin.

Brandtstädter, S. (2007). Transitional spaces: Postsocialism as a cultural process. *Critique of Anthropology, 27*(2), 131–45.

Cohen, M. L. (2005). *Kinship, contract, community, and state: Anthropological perspectives on China.* Stanford, CA: Stanford University Press.

Comaroff, J. & Comaroff, J. L. (Eds.) (2006). *Law and disorder in the postcolony.* Chicago, IL: University of Chicago Press.

Cowan, J. K., Dembour, M-B. & Wilson, R. A. (Eds.) (2001). *Culture and rights: Anthropological perspectives.* Cambridge, Cambridge University Press.

Engerman, S. L. & Sokoloff, K. L. (2005). The evolution of suffrage institutions in the New World. *Journal of Economic History, 65*(4), 891–921.

Fong, V. L. & Murphy, R. (Eds.) (2006). *Chinese citizenship: Views from the margin.* London and New York: Routledge.

Habermas, J. (2000). Struggles for recognition in the democratic constitutional state. In J. Habermas, C. Cronin & P. De Greiff (Eds.), *The inclusion of the other: Studies in political theory* (pp. 203–36). Cambridge, MA: MIT Press.

Hale, C. R. (2002). Does multiculturalism menace? Governance, cultural rights and the politics of identity in Guatemala. *Journal of Latin American Studies, 34*, 485–524.

Hale, C. R. (2005). Neoliberal multiculturalism: The remaking of cultural rights and racial dominance in Central America. *PoLAR: Political and Legal Anthropology Review, 28*(1), 10–28.

Harvey, D. (2005). *A brief history of neoliberalism.* New York: Oxford University Press.

Holston, J. (2008). *Insurgent citizenship: Disjunctions of democracy and modernity in Brazil*. Princeton, NJ: Princeton University Press.

Kandiyoti, D. (2000). Modernization without the market? The case of the 'Soviet East'. In A. Arce & N. Long (Eds.), *Anthropology, development and modernities: Exploring discourse, counter-tendencies and violence* (pp. 52–63). London: Routledge.

Marshall, T. H. (1964). *Class, citizenship and social development*. Cambridge: Cambridge University Press.

Mehta, U. S. (1997). Liberal strategies of exclusion. In F. Cooper & A. L. Stoler (Eds.), *Tensions of empire: Colonial cultures in a bourgeois world* (pp. 59–86). Berkeley: University of California Press.

Mill, J. S. (1929 [1869]). *The subjection of women*. London: Dent.

Mill, J. S. (1975 [1859]). *On liberty*. New York: Norton.

Ong, A. (1999). Cultural citizenship as subject-making: Immigrants negotiate racial and cultural boundaries in the United States. In R. D. Torres, L. F. Mirón & J. X. Inda (Eds.), *Race, identity and citizenship: A reader* (pp. 262–93). Oxford: Blackwell.

Passavant, P. A. (1996). A moral geography of liberty: John Stuart Mill and American free speech discourse. *Social Legal Studies*, 5(3), 301–20.

Rosaldo, R. (1999). Cultural citizenship, inequality and multiculturalism. In R. D. Torres, L. F. Mirón & J. X. Inda (Eds.), *Race, identity and citizenship: A reader* (pp. 253–61). Oxford: Blackwell.

Rose, N. (1999). *Powers of freedom: Reframing political thought*. Cambridge: Cambridge University Press.

Rose, N. & Miller, P. (2008). *Governing the present: Administering economic, social and personal life*. Cambridge: Polity.

Sandel, M. J. (1984). The procedural republic and the unencumbered self. *Political Theory*, 12(1), 81–96.

Santos, B. de Souza. (2005). Beyond neoliberal governance: The World Social Forum as subaltern cosmopolitan politics and legality. In B. de Souza Santos & C. Rodríguez-Garavito (Eds.), *Law and globalization from below: Towards a cosmopolitan legality* (pp. 29–63). Cambridge: Cambridge University Press.

Taylor, C. & Gutmann, A. (1994). *Multiculturalism and 'the politics of recognition'*. Princeton, NJ: Princeton University Press.

Van Cott, D. L. (2000). *The friendly liquidation of the past: The politics of diversity in Latin America*. Pittsburgh, PA: University of Pittsburgh Press.

Wade, P. (Ed.) (2000). *The right to difference is a fundamental human right: GDAT debates*. Manchester: Group for Debates in Anthropological Theory.

Wade, P. (2005). Rethinking *mestizaje*: Ideology and lived experience. *Journal of Latin American Studies*, 37, 1–19.

Wang, J. (1996). *High culture fever: Politics, aesthetics, and ideology in Deng's China*. Berkeley: University of California Press.

Wilson, R. A. (Ed.) (1996). *Human rights, culture and context: Anthropological perspectives*. London: Pluto Press.

Woodward, K. A. (2007). On and off the pitch: Diversity policies and transforming identities. *Cultural Studies*, 21(4–5), 758–78.

Woodward, K. A. (2009). *Embodied sporting practices: Regulating and regulatory bodies*. Basingstoke: Palgrave Macmillan.

Yuval-Davis, N. & Werbner, P. (Eds.) (1999). *Women, citizenship and difference*. London: Zed Books.

Zhang, L. & Ong, A. (Eds.) (2008). *Privatizing China: Socialism from afar*. Ithaca, NY: Cornell University Press.

Žižek, S (1997). Multiculturalism, or, the cultural logic of multinational capitalism. *New Left Review*, 1(225), 1–15.

Resistencia para que? Territory, autonomy and neoliberal entanglements in the 'empty spaces' of Central America

Charles R. Hale

Abstract

This paper explores black and indigenous land rights struggles in Central America, focusing especially on the contradictions produced and deepened by strategies of neoliberal governance. Paradoxically, among the most daunting obstacles is not repression or denial of rights, but, rather, partial recognition and the bureaucratic-political entanglements that follow. Another major challenge is the declining viability of agrarian development in the globalized Central American political economy. The second part of the paper reflects critically on recent attempts to understand these problems, through the practice of politically engaged anthropological scholarship. Activist research, I argue, draws the anthropologist into some of the same contradictions and predicaments that the actors themselves confront. While this makes for difficulties at various levels, it can also be a privileged source of insight and analytical enrichment.

More than a decade has passed since Latin American states turned multi-cultural. In a dramatic reversal of the pattern established during the previous century and half of nation-building, broad affirmations of cultural pluralism, and of culturally differentiated citizenship rights, are now the rule.[1] The curious paradox whereby the rise of multiculturalism has coincided with an equally widespread turn to neoliberal economic reform has preoccupied me for some time. Along with many others, I have tried to think about how these two processes work together, yielding a conjoined regime of governance (see, for example, Hale, 2002; Hale & Millaman, 2006; Postero, 2007; Rivera Cusicanqui, 2004; Speed, 2008). Until recently, however, I viewed Afro-indigenous struggles for land and resource rights as marking the outer limits of this paradox. If black and indigenous communities demand *collective* rights to territory, insist that land is *not* a commodity, that their rights are *antecedent* to the formation of the nation-state, do these claims not present a frontal challenge to the precepts of neoliberalism? Might we even portray these struggles for territory – whose outcome in many cases is still uncertain – as a critical juncture in the history of neoliberal governance in Latin America, a gauge of people's ability to resist and, even, to turn the tide?

This article reflects on a series of activist research projects in Central America, begun a decade ago, that took the answers to these questions to be 'yes'. The research has been adamantly collective, involving teams of university-based geographers, lawyers and anthropologists, as well as intellectuals who belong to the communities and organizations in struggle for their rights. It has been conceived, from the start, to generate scholarly insight while at the same time yielding results that are immediately useful to the protagonists of these struggles.[2] Most recently these efforts involved a three-country study funded by the Ford Foundation, in which a steering committee composed of university- and civil society-based intellectuals chose four sites where the research would be carried out. In each site high-stakes struggles for land rights are under way; in each site leaders portray these struggles as movements of resistance against the neoliberal onslaught. The project's central challenge was to produce knowledge that advances these ends; my task here is to take stock of the entire process, reflecting on what we achieved and what we learned from the research, while also attending to the contradictions that these efforts brought to the fore.[3]

The first of the four sites is Tucurú, a *municipio* (township) in the department of Alta Vera Paz, Guatemala, which until recently consisted entirely of large coffee farms (or *fincas*) owned by Euro-Guatemalan elites. In the early 1990s the peasant rights organization *Coordinadora Nacional Indígena y Campesina* (CONIC) joined efforts with *finca* workers – most of whom are monolingual Q'eqchi' Mayas – to regain their lands, taken from them a century before (Hurtado Paz y Paz, 2008; Macleod Howland, 1997; Padilla *et al.*, 2007). The basic strategy – to organize occupations of the fincas, sue the owners for underpayment of wages and benefits, then to negotiate devolution of *finca* land in lieu of repayment – turned out to be remarkably successful. By 2006 some sixty Maya communities had achieved legalized or quasi-legalized rights to roughly one-third of Tucuru's territory. Our research, culminating in the summer of 2007, focused on changing land tenure, gender relations and economic alternatives throughout the *municipio*, and especially in the former Finca Cuchil, recently occupied and still not legally owned by the workers. The luxurious *casa patronal*, guarded 24-7 by its former workers, became the logistical base for our research team. During a visit to the site in June 2007, I awoke early one morning to speak with a young man who had just finished his night shift as guard of the *casa patronal*. We looked up a hillside covered with coffee that this year they would organize to harvest themselves. 'Gradually', he told me, 'it is beginning to feel like this land is really ours'.

Two of the other three sites are located in Honduras, and the third in Nicaragua. On the north coast of Honduras we worked with fifteen communities of the Afro-indigenous Garífuna people, in struggle to claim the Iriona territory, in conjunction with an organization representing them called OFRANEH.[4] In the Moskitia farther to the east our research centred around the Miskitu Indian town of Mokorón, in alliance with the Miskitu organization 'Unified People of the Moskitia' (MASTA). In Nicaragua we teamed up with the autonomous university URACCAN and the multiracial territorial commission of Pearl Lagoon. Although these three struggles have distinct histories, their vision of territorial rights and the research they requested in support of this vision took similar forms. They all claimed multicommunal blocs (known as *bloques*), which encompassed territory and resources belonging to a cluster of some ten to fifteen communities. In each case they needed maps, legal and historical arguments, and ethnographic evidence that would bolster their assertions that this land, which they have traditionally used and occupied, should actually become their property. A key point of reference in these assertions was a pair of recent studies, funded by the World Bank, which affirm the *bloque* form of land demarcation and provide a rough cut of the boundaries between one *bloque* and the next. The Nicaraguan study was completed in 1998 and the Honduran Moskitia study in 2002 (see Figures 1 and 2). By the time our current research on these four sites began in 2005, what geographer Karl Offen (2003) calls the 'territorial turn' – that is, the inclination of both Latin American states and multilateral development institutions to recognize black and indigenous demands for territory – was already well under way (see also Gros, n.d.).

In March of 2007 we convened a workshop, where participants in each of these struggles came together to discuss challenges and strategies. At one memorable moment in the discussion, an Afro-Nicaraguan mentioned the possibility of soliciting World Bank support for the final phase of efforts to gain legal title to the Pearl Lagoon territory. This suggestion had a straightforward rationale. In all four sites of struggle, the World Bank has supported the territorial turn. At the same time, the terms of this support have been deeply contradictory: in some respects opening space for Afro-indigenous territorial rights, in other respects setting limits on the reach of these claims. Among Garífuna communities, these limiting effects had been especially troublesome. OFRANEH was locked in conflict with the World Bank-funded Land Administration Project (or PATH), which had offered to title Garífuna lands, while also supporting major plans under way for large-scale tourist development along the spectacular Caribbean

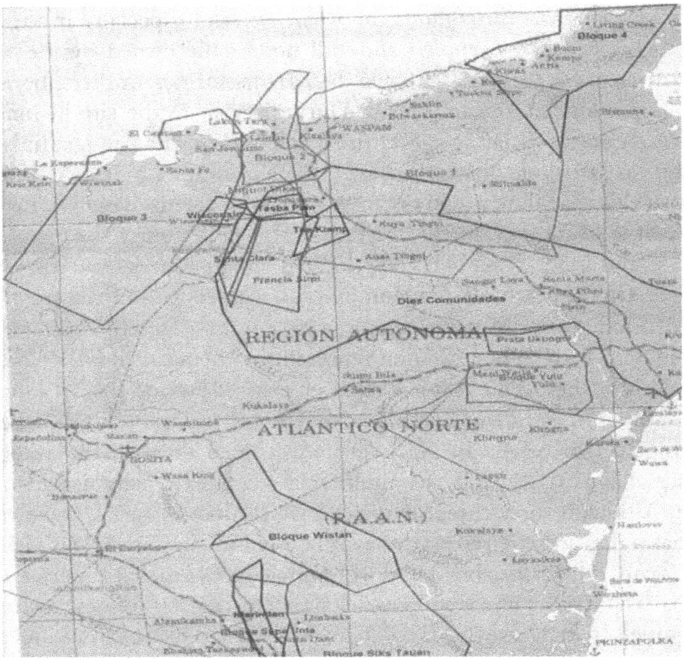

Figure 1 CCARC land rights study results in northeastern Nicaragua

coastline that Garífuna communities occupy. With this conflict in mind Marta, a sharp and outspoken activist intellectual from OFRANEH, gently redirected the Afro-Nicaraguan's suggestion:

> we have values that are not negotiable – our relationship with the land is one example. This topic is not an academic matter. It is a matter of our collective existence as a people. . . . These values are our great source of strength. We have to know what we are struggling for, *resistencia para que?* We do many things that are incomprehensible to the western world; there is a great chasm between us. Before talking with [the World Bank], we have to ask ourselves some basic questions, starting with the most important: do we want to survive as a people?

Marta's intervention pre-empted further discussion of the matter. The common thread in all four struggles, after all, is collective rights to territory, and the established discourse that justifies these rights is radical cultural difference in opposition to the homogenizing, neoliberal development policies epitomized by the World Bank.

Activist research methods ask that we give priority to the research products that the struggle in question requires, which in turn requires judicious use of our well-honed tools of deconstruction and cultural critique. Such restraint is

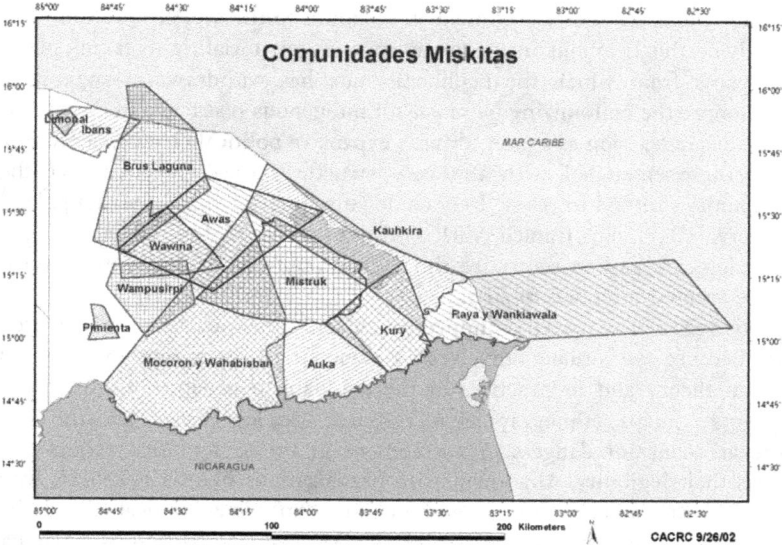

Figure 2 CCARC land rights study results, Honduran Moskitia, 2002

challenging given the multiple provocations embedded in Marta's intervention. There is the telltale assumption of sedentary metaphysics,[5] the assertion of a (very unpostmodern sounding) stark divide between indigenous and Westerns ways, the indigenous wisdom trope, even more tantalizing since the Garífuna claim indigeneity from an interpellated subject position of blackness.[6] Leaving all this deconstructive probing aside for the moment, I would like to take up Marta's challenge. *Resistencia para que?* is an especially apt question, because its meaning changes with intonation. In one phrasing – *para que?* what's the use – it can express a typical neoliberal admonition; Marta surely meant it differently, calling our attention to urgent tactical priorities, while perhaps alluding to an expansive, even utopian, political horizon as well. Two analytical puzzles follow. To what extent can black and indigenous territorial rights advance within the broader logic of neoliberal development in Central America? When these peoples struggle for rights to territory, what are the ends of their resistance and how do we make sense of the divergence between these ends and the results that their efforts yield?

In response to the first question, I argue that we are observing the early stages of emergence of a new state form – not withdrawal, not even 'armed retreat', as Leslie Gill (2000) has depicted the contradictory effects of neoliberal reform in Bolivia – but, rather, a proactive and productive reconfiguration. In Central America the neoliberal state has largely abandoned pretensions of national territorial encompassment, adopting instead a spatially differentiated logic that directs resources – productive and coercive – towards certain economically favoured areas, leaving other areas and their inhabitants to fend for themselves. My argument in response to the second question builds directly on this troubling image, of advances in territorial rights taking place in the spaces from which the neoliberal state has withdrawn. I suggest that 'autonomy', the epitomizing '*para que*' of indigenous resistance in the previous era, is losing traction as a path towards expansive political change, because it is increasingly entangled with the very structures of dominance that these communities intend to resist. I conclude searching for signs that struggles for territory might be framed differently, to contain the effects of these entanglements and to recapture the radical political imaginary that Marta's phrase seemed intended to spark.

Activist research is well equipped to address these puzzles of the territorial turn because we situate ourselves in their midst, engaging them directly both in theory and in practice. In the mandate to generate useful research products – maps, ethnographies of resource use, legal briefs and the like – there are constant dangers of entrapment in the system that requires and judges their legibility. Alignment with organizations like OFRANEH, whose leaders voice radical critiques and nurture expansive political alternatives, keeps this sense of entrapment in check. Yet such organizations often have trouble meeting the immediate, practical needs of their members, given the complicity with the neoliberal establishment that this generally entails. The disjuncture between these two sensibilities and organizational cultures – one of radical anti-systemic critique and the other of pragmatic daily problem solving – is disconcerting and at times frankly debilitating.[7] Experience-based analysis of this disjuncture, in turn, brings a third overarching argument to the fore. One of the great ideological achievements of 'the neoliberal grand slam' of the 1990s – to borrow Perry Anderson's (2000) provocative phrase – has been to sever the link between these two sensibilities, or, rather, to create incentives and pressures that induce us to sever the link ourselves. I apply this argument both to the land rights struggles themselves and to the theoretical tools we have developed to understand them. It is commonplace to portray neoliberal hegemony as suppressing anti-systemic critique and censuring radical alternatives. Its more debilitating effect, in my view, is to discourage the *creative articulation* between these utopian sensibilities and the always compromised, always urgent, struggles for relief from oppression and for modest material wellbeing in the here and now.

The neoliberal state and its 'empty spaces'

Capitalist expansion in Central America since the nineteenth century has advanced through the conquest of land and resources portrayed as underused, misused or just plain empty. The Caribbean coast of Nicaragua offers the classic case of this mode of neocolonial conquest, punctuated by forceful annexation, which state actors justified by representing Indians as woefully uncivilized and blacks as foreigners who did not belong.[8] Enclave production of bananas in the north coast region of Honduras followed a similar logic. Destabilized by the immense power of northern capital and US geopolitical presence, these states could not exercise control over their own territories, except as junior partners in someone else's business deal (Euraque, 1998). State elites, when they did find their voice and footing, deployed ideologies that followed the pattern of what Gupta and Ferguson (2002) call 'encompassment': control the territory, establish vertical lines of authority, confer liberal citizenship rights that in theory include everyone but in practice reinforce race–class hierarchies and assert temporal narratives of national development.[9]

By the second half of the twentieth century this drive for encompassment in the isthmus had achieved highly uneven results, limited by external factors and by its own internal contradictions. With the partial exception of Guatemala's reformist government of 1944–54, effective projects of encompassment did not congeal in any of the three countries until the rise of armed conflict in the 1980s. In Guatemala this took the form of a genocidal counter-insurgency campaign, which inflicted terror and trauma on indigenous communities through the highlands.[10] Virtual occupation of Honduras by US armed forces in the 1980s limited the Honduran state's reach, especially in the Moskitia, but the US withdrawal at the decade's end left a fortified Honduran army and a renewed impetus for nationalization of its territory.[11] In Nicaragua, the Sandinistas fashioned an especially assertive, Left-inflected version of the territorial state, which nettled incipient indigenous and Afro-Nicaraguan rights movements, while also raising their collective expectations. This combination proved explosive. With ample funding from the US, civic resistance gave way to armed struggle; black and indigenous organizations waged a guerrilla war against the Sandinistas with demands for autonomy at front and centre. After adamant refusal for four years, the Sandinistas relented, and enacted a profoundly ambivalent policy turn: regional autonomy for the Atlantic Coast region was in part auto-critique and visionary advance in black and indigenous rights, but in part also precocious experiment with multiculturalism as containment.

In the years after the Sandinistas lost the national elections in 1990, processes of neoliberal development enveloped both Nicaragua and Honduras, gradually displacing the ideology of temporal-territorial encompassment. Both regions of the Moskitia, still relatively resource-rich in precious lumber, minerals and undeveloped coastal lands, became sites of contention between foreign companies, which paid the cash-starved states up front for potentially lucrative concessions. The iconic case of this conflict occurred in northeastern Nicaragua, where the indigenous (Mayangna) community of Awas Tingni squared off against the state in an eight-year legal battle for land rights, which ended up in the Inter-American Human Rights Court. Government spokespeople opposed the claim with rhetoric that remained firmly embedded in the previous era: the state's prerogatives over its own empty spaces and the mandate to civilize Indians by bringing them into the temporal flow of national development (Anaya & Grossman, 2002; Bryan, 2007; Hale, 2006a). But the court's ruling – echoing the Awas Tingni counsel's formidable legal argument that a truly modern state must recognize cultural diversity – endorsed the emergent principle: collective rights to territory justified by traditional occupancy and indigenous cultural difference. While neoliberal elites in Nicaragua were divided on this multi-cultural turn – from bitter resistance to cautious support – their corruption, fragmentation and at times utter incompetence amplified the influence of powerful external actors such as the Inter-American Court and the World Bank, in moving that very agenda forward.

During the 1990s Honduras experienced the same entangled emergence of neoliberal multiculturalism. Neoliberal reforms were epitomized by the notorious Congressional Decree 90-90, an amendment to Article #107 of the Constitution passed in 1990, which made it legal for foreigners to own beach land, thereby clearing the way for a surge of beach-side property sales and mega-tourist development.[12] Black and indigenous organizations in this period engaged in intense protest and mobilization. The pan-ethnic organization called COMPAH, formed in the early 1990s, acted on behalf of nine distinct organizations with a remarkably unified voice, in favour of multi-cultural reforms, against neoliberal megaprojects, such as the proposal to dam the Patuca River.[13] Over the next fifteen years the state begrudgingly conceded a series of key multicultural reforms: signing on to ILO Convention 169 (1995), passing a property law that allows for multicommunal land claims (June 2004), initiating the World Bank-funded land administration project (PATH), which purports to support black and indigenous claims (2004).[14]

In Guatemala, the transition to state multiculturalism began soon after the return to democratic rule in the late 1980s, but with agrarian relations and land rights as the non-negotiable taboo. Important and substantive reforms of the state followed, in nearly all the areas specified by the Indigenous chapter of the 1996 Peace Accords: language, education, spirituality and the like. Then, beginning in the late 1990s, a wave of *finca* occupations, like those in Tucurú, swept the country. To the surprise of many observers, rather than calling in the army, the government allowed many of these occupations to happen. In part, the explanation lay in the anti-oligarchic leanings of Alfonso Portillo, the president at the time, and his party the FRG. However, Portillo's ambivalence concealed a more basic truth: the coffee market was ailing and *finqueros* generally preferred to re-invest their capital elsewhere. Although jittery about the challenge to private property, they were thrilled to have the Guatemalan state use funds provided by the World Bank for 'market-driven land reform' to buy them out.

The Central America-wide spatial distribution of these country-specific patterns calls out for attention. Consider, for example, the map that inadvertently inspired the subtitle of this article, presented in a recent seminar on Central America's new model of economic development (Figure 3). Although meant only to depict the infrastructural underpinnings of contemporary patterns of capital investment, and missing a few data points at that, the stark spatial dichotomy frames the argument nicely. The areas of economic dynamism in these increasingly urbanized countries are the principal cities,

Figure 3 Pacific corridor of Central America

the strips along the highways that connect these cities to one another, to their principal ports and to a half-dozen major nodes of enclave tourism. Beyond these areas, the map may as well be empty, not in the literal demographic sense, but in that neither the people nor the places play important roles in the newly globalized economy. Although export agriculture remains important in some parts of Central America, it is no longer the mainstay. Salvadoran economist Alexander Segovia uses the term 'structural break' to signal the profound shift in the sources of economic dynamism toward globally articulated sectors such as maquila production, financial services, construction, remittance-driven commerce and the like, to which the empty spaces contribute very little (Programa de Apoyo a la Integración Regional Centroamericana, 2003; Segovia, 2005). Two striking aggregate statistical changes, depicted in Tables 1 and 2, stand in as a promissory note on a fuller, spatially differentiated mapping of these new economic relations: a drop in Central America-wide agricultural production, from 30 to 16 per cent of the GNP over the past three decades, and the complete displacement of coffee by maquilas, tourism and remittances as the principal sources of foreign exchange. The major apparent exception in the spatial pattern – enclave tourism – ends up reinforcing the rule. Afro-indigenous communities participate, but mainly as sources of reserve labour, cultural attractions or, at best, as small community-controlled enterprises that operate on the margins.[15] In sum, Segovia's notion of a structural break – basically a temporal frame to mark the changing configuration of

25

Table 1 Structure of the Gross Domestic Product in Central America (percentages)

	1970	1980	1990	2000	2004
Agricultural sector	30.4	26.8	18.9	16.7	16.2
Industrial sector	22.0	23.4	21.0	22.1	21.6
Services	40.1	40.4	53.4	55.3	57.3
Government services	7.6	9.4	6.6	5.6	4.9

Source: Segovia (2005).

productive relations – has a largely unexamined spatial logic with far-reaching political consequences for black and indigenous politics.

Economically, these 'empty spaces' become grey zones, which sequentially or even simultaneously encompass both fabulous profits from unregulated economic activity and the constant threat of economic breakdown due to the absence of effective state presence. James Ferguson (2006) has elucidated the former scenario using case material from Africa, in an elegant inversion of the standard assumption that ungoverned spaces are bad for business. In Central America, this pattern is nicely exemplified by drug sale and trans-shipment, which thrive in the empty spaces, and, also, by the booming illegal and semi-legal lumber industry. Evidence of the second scenario – economic breakdown – is also widespread, especially where there is a combination of greater local control and strong patterns of local political mobilization. Devolution of political authority and minimal state presence contribute directly to what commentators refer to as the problem of 'ungovernability' (*ingobernabilidad*) in many highland Maya *municipios*: with inadequate resources and increased responsibilities to confront the overwhelming challenges of structural poverty, Maya-controlled local governments with newfound 'autonomy' end up mired in self-generated conflict.[16] A similar pattern prevails in northeast Nicaragua, which has been home to three separate armed insurgencies since 1990 and a constant flow of local militant protest.[17] Even along the international border between Nicaragua and Honduras – once

Table 2 Principal sources of foreign exchange in Central America (percentages; partial list)

	1990	1995	2000	2004
Coffee	18.1	15.8	8.8	4.7
Maquila	2.6	5.3	14.6	13
Remittances	12.7	15	16.9	32.6
Tourism	8.8	9.8	12.8	14.5

Source: Segovia (2005).

a major site of geopolitical contention – state presence is threadbare and community development efforts, if present at all, are the purview of internationally funded NGOs.

Whether by design or the force of circumstance, the structural break is yielding a reconfiguration of governance in these empty spaces: less effort to locate inhabitants within temporal narratives of progress and to assert authority over them in the name of national-territorial encompassment, a more instrumental state presence, to maintain order and reap benefits in relation to particular economic initiatives; otherwise a surprising receptivity to the devolution of political-economic power. Instead of territorial encompassment, the neoliberal state has embraced practices of spatially differentiated rule: nodes of dynamism that require active political-economic presence, in juxtaposition to large spaces that are rendered essentially redundant. Political scientist Guillermo O'Donnell (1999), in reference to post-authoritarian Latin America more generally, has analysed this spatially differentiated terrain using the metaphor of a heat map: blue splotches where the rule of law functions reasonably well, green areas where the state is minimally present, and vast expanses of brown, where both presence and efficacy are minimal to nil. The next piece in the puzzle is to make the 'heat map' attentive to racial difference, noting the high percentage of black and indigenous peoples who occupy these brown areas, and thinking through the political consequences.

O'Donnell's metaphor serves this purpose to a point, but contains a misleading Weberian assumption of a direct linear relationship between formal state presence and governmental effects. The US government security apparatus, especially in the post-9/11 world, inadvertently questions that assumption. Defense Department scholar Martin Edwin Andersen (2006), for example, worries a lot about the brown areas (which he calls 'ungoverned spaces'), arguing that they are prime breeding grounds for terrorists. This threat is best exemplified for him by the Chiapas rebellion and the associated trend towards Muslim conversion among disaffected Maya. His solution sounds disconcertingly progressive. The US should make friends with the Indians who occupy these 'ungoverned spaces', supporting their territorial rights and demands for autonomy to fill the breach. This line of reasoning can only reinforce the Latin America-wide shift towards state recognition of Afro-indigenous collective property rights. The data recently compiled by the Colombian legal scholar Roque Roldán (2005) are truly astounding: in Costa Rica 6 per cent of national territory has been turned over to indigenous and Afro-descendant peoples, Ecuador 10 per cent, Brazil 12 per cent, Panamá 20 per cent and Colombia 30 per cent. How could a demand that for so long touched a chord of visceral opposition from Latin American elites, now find such strong support in the higher echelons of the neoliberal establishment and at least ambivalent assent by the states themselves?

Although neoliberal reforms and Afro-indigenous land rights often do stand in tension, there are conditions under which the two can complement and reinforce one another. Multilateral development institutions like the World

Bank and the IDB are solidly behind their own preferred versions of both trends. With one hand, they promote multimillion dollar projects in each Central American country that seek to 'modernize' land registries, extending the grid of market intelligibility in property rights regimes throughout the region. With bank blessings and support, these states have reformed and rehabilitated national laws that facilitate large-scale mining, beach-side tourist development and a veritable explosion in the international market for relatively cheap, undeveloped Central American properties. With the other hand, the banks reach out to indigenous and black peoples, with special programmes in support of their land and resource rights. In Nicaragua, direct World Bank pressure, combined with fortuitous national political conditions, helped Nicaraguan Costeños to achieve Law 445, the most expansive legislation in Latin America for the demarcation of community lands (see Goett, 2006; Gonzalez, 2008). A few years later, responding to similar pressure, the Honduran state passed the *Ley de Propiedad*, which exudes ambivalence but at least opens the door for multicommunal indigenous land rights.[18] The more timid parallel move in Guatemala was the World Bank-financed *Fondo de Tierras*, which extends loans to peasants, helping them buy the land of large landowners who, for their own reasons, want out. Community-based land rights fit within broader efforts to regularize land tenure and to establish clear rules by which all actors – whether individuals or communities – can turn their resources into commodities.

The stated rationale for this transformation is compensatory justice, while further probing brings a more hard-nosed economic logic to the fore. The compensatory justice argument is summed up with the phrase 'development with identity', which embraces a chain of assertions: modern states recognize cultural difference; indigenous peoples need special regimes of rights that help them to negotiate the rigors of modernity; without such provisions, these peoples would lose their culture.[19] An implicit economic rationale underlies this apparent benevolence. Even if large swaths of territory are excluded from the land market, regularization of land tenure pays off, both because the rest of the land becomes fair game for commoditization and because the existence of collectively owned property poses no direct challenge to the principle of private property or to the reign of market forces, but does achieve the key goal of replacing chaos and contention with an intelligible, predictable and market-friendly grid of property rights. These two principles together – special rights and reinforcement of a capitalist market for land and resources – converge to yield an especially compelling logic: states devolve authority to far-flung spaces, recognize the inhabitants' rights and let them govern themselves, which has the effect of constraining their political participation beyond the local level, especially in relation to broader structures of political-economic inequity. Meanwhile, this devolution forms part of the overall recognition of multicultural rights, which generates an array of attractive quasi-governmental jobs that the most able leaders of these rights struggles are constantly recruited to fill.[20]

This scenario, amply present in Central America, requires us to imbue our thinking about neoliberal governance with a more explicitly spatial dimension. Depending on the character of the locale, the governance regime can vary widely, even within the purview of a single nation-state. In areas of high economic priority such as tourist enclaves and free trade zones, for example, the state leaves little to chance, relying on a battery of regulations and prohibitions enforced with immediate recourse to coercive power. In the 'brown' areas that are metaphorically 'empty', governance occurs more through self-regulating mechanisms: the rules and procedures that communities must follow in order to reap the benefits of their own resources; the mayor of a rural 'autonomous' *municipio* who exercises authority in the name of the state, when institutions of the state proper are nowhere to be found. There are of course many variations between these two extremes, distinguished by a number of factors, most prominently the differential presence of NGOs and quasi-state organizations, which practise self-regulation that is convergent with but largely autonomous from the specific governance regime of the state. Spatial differentiation of governance, in short, is not principally about gradations between 'more' and 'less', but, rather, about differentiated *logics*, produced by variation in the presence of key constituent parts such as state coercion, locally grounded state policies, NGOs and local authorities. In this light it becomes possible that the state can devolve authority to the local level, through carefully crafted regimes of autonomy, while continuing to achieve key neoliberal governance outcomes through alternative means.

By using the word 'logic' I do not mean to suggest that the transformation has been linear, seamless or systematically planned from above. Political-ideological remnants of the territorial state remain strong, expressed in visceral fears of autonomy and opposition to any notion of collective land rights. Concrete advances in line with the territorial turn have generally occurred in an atmosphere of pitched battles with uncertain outcomes, often with multilateral institutions weighing in to tip the balance. A common, if somewhat bizarre, feature of these battles is the grumbling by elite opponents of the territorial turn about World Bank 'imperialism' in favour of indigenous peoples.[21] The most volatile element in this contradictory brew is the resistance movements themselves: partly enabled by neoliberal reforms, partly driven by radical anti-systemic critique; deeply divided on how to claim the spaces opened by neoliberal multiculturalism without succumbing to their built-in limits.

Between the romance of resistance and the conceit of govermentality

Conquest of these so-called empty spaces since the nineteenth century has generally accentuated identity-based resistance among those who lived there. This pattern has long been apparent in the Honduran and Nicaraguan Moskitia, where these movements hark back to the quasi-independent governmental status they enjoyed until 1894 as subjects of the British crown (Hale, 1994). A recent revisionist history of Guatemala makes a parallel point, showing how the state's *de facto* 'separate and unequal' policies laid the historical groundwork for contemporary Maya cultural rights activism.[22] These resistance movements, in turn, have played a central role in pushing the states to recognize multicultural rights. Our theoretical work on neoliberal multiculturalism remains seriously deficient if it does not take this resistance fully into account. My own ethnographic research among provincial *ladino* elites in Guatemala, for example, led me to worry about this rise of multicultural recognition as a political menace: allowing leaders to affirm cultural equality while also retaining racial privilege (Hale, 2006b). But simultaneous work with land rights movements keeps this line of analysis in check, providing a constant reminder of the material gains they can achieve, of the substantive rights they can push the state to grant and of the utopian promise that they keep alive. Without such reminders, analyses of govern-mentality can all too easily slip into a scholarly conceit, the flip side of what Abu-Lughod (1990) rightly criticized as the 'romance of resistance'. We all have read Foucault and Nikolas Rose; we know how power works; what activists portray as resistance is best understood as constrained manoeuvrings, which at best yield a range of unstable, fluid and ambiguous effects.

The energy of these four land rights struggles is too intense, their relations with dominant actors too volatile and their irreverence towards academic knowledge too great to allow this conceit to stand. Granted, they face contradictions at every turn, both of the theoretically resonant variety, invoked by the phrase neoliberal multiculturalism, and others at times involving more mundane issues of authoritarian leadership styles, mismanagement of funds, organizational deficiencies and the like. But they also consistently push at the limits of what the neoliberal state will allow and they periodically generate flashes of vision for political transformation. My analytical task in this second section of the article is to trace the tension between these substantive advances towards collective empowerment and the ongoing entanglements with relations of inequality, in hopes of thinking through the issues at stake in Marta's question, '*resistencia para que?*'

In Tucurú the juxtaposition is especially jarring: utopian possibilities alongside a sense of utter entrapment in political-economic relations that leave very little room for manoeuvre. The story line has an epic feel. Monolingual indigenous families are tied to the *fincas* as '*mozos colonos*', a distinctively Guatemalan labour form that approaches serfdom. They gain their freedom and their land, bursting into the twenty-first century with revolutionary fervour, having leapt several centuries in a single decade. This image of abrupt reversal turns positively surreal in the places where 'recuperation' of the *fincas* has included the *casa patronal*, complete with swimming pools and stately dining rooms, the walls still adorned with the *finquero*'s perverse tastes in interior design: deer-head trophies and tourist kitsch prints of Maya women. Yet the challenges of putting this 'recuperated' land to use are multiple and daunting. Having lived largely cut off from broadly circulating discourses of indigeneity, these Q'eqchi' Maya tend to pose demands as former wage-workers who are soon to become small-holding peasants. In some cases, an ethos of collectivity borne in struggle has prevailed in the organization of production afterwards; in others families have demanded individual land titles, to the dismay of CONIC organizers, who view the process as integral to a broader vision of indigenous empowerment. Once in control of the land, whether as collective or individual owners, the liberated workers must engage a globalized agricultural economy, in which even their former *patrones* found it difficult to compete, in many cases having assumed crushing levels of debt in return for the land. CONIC's strong suits are political mobilization and national-level negotiation for Maya empowerment, not grassroots productive alternatives.[23] Drawing on prior dialogue with CONIC leaders, our activist research team settled into the newly recuperated Finca Cuchil with a mandate to gauge progress towards an inspiring – and decidedly utopian – political horizon: the autonomous Q'eqchi' *municipio* of Tucurú. Without directly contradicting this ideal, leaders of the *Comité Agropecuario Cuchil* added a more immediate research question: what would it take to turn their ex-*finca* into an eco-tourist enterprise?

In the Moskitia of Honduras, also, the struggle for rights to territory bears a direct relationship to a broader politics of indigenous empowerment. Perhaps more than in Tucurú, the utopian horizon of our research resonated with pretty much everyone. In virtually any collective discussion of land rights, one can expect a Miskitu elder to rise and paint the picture of territorial rights in vivid, quasi-millenarian rhetoric. For example, the collectively produced document, written first in Miskitu then translated into Spanish, which served as the framework for the Mokorón mapping initiative begins:

Moskitia Indianka ai raitka turka ba. a. Jesús kau balras kan taim, Indian uplikanani pat Moskitiara iwi kan. b. Anduras gabamint aisubi takan taim, Indian ai raitka nani bara kan, sakuna, warbi tikaia trai kaiki kan, la raya mihta. c. Baha mita Moskitia lupia nani ai raitkaia dukiara asla taki bawan, MASTA asla Takanka dauki bangwan, 1976 manka. d. Naiwa kat ban ai klabi bangwisa ai raitkara bara ai tasbaia dukiara

The indigenous people of the Moskitia have historic rights. a. When Jesus Christ arrived to this earth, the indigenous people were already living in the Moskitia. b. When the government of Honduras was founded, indigenous people already had rights, but the government created new laws with the intention of eliminating those rights. c. In order to defend those rights, the sons and daughters of the Moskitia founded MASTA in 1976. d. Our struggle for rights to land and resources continues to this day.

The reasoning leads to the irrefutable conclusion that 'the whole Moskitia belongs to us', even if no one has a plan for achieving this expansive demand, especially in the face of a state that until recently had been viscerally hostile to any notion of indigenous autonomy. By the beginning of this century MASTA leaders had settled on the strategy of claiming multicommunal *bloques*, with territories that correspond to the ten federations that make up the Moskitia-wide organization. Our research team received the mandate to document the first of these ten territorial claims, that of a federation called FINZMOS. Participatory cartographic, legal and ethnographic research came together to produce a comprehensive analysis of the territory, which in turn laid the groundwork for a legal petition, submitted to the Honduran Agrarian Reform Ministry in mid-October 2007.

We still do not know how state elites will respond to this demand or what the consequences of their eventual response will be. There is little chance that they will accede completely, but, regardless, having title to a territory is sure to strengthen their negotiating position. Moreover, in the face of dire threats to the FINZMOS communities' resource base – from impoverished peasant migrants, large-scale venture capitalists and the state itself – secure collective land rights are an indispensable first step, an immediate objective on which most everyone agrees. Yet many doubts remain. The multicommunal territory would be governed by some form of autonomous Miskitu political institution, which would assume weighty responsibility for the management of local affairs, according to rules that the state undoubtedly would continue to influence from a distance. Given MASTA's frankly weak organizational foundations, the abundant potential for state manipulation, the abject poverty of the communities that comprise the ten federations and the threatening presence of third-party inhabitants inside the territory, immediate achievement of substantial powers of self-government could be disastrous. We presented the finished product to an appreciative gathering of MASTA and FINZMOS leaders in June 2007, and they vowed to forge ahead to achieve definitive title of the territory. Afterwards, I had the uneasy sense that the Honduran state could best thwart the broader movement for Miskitu empowerment not by denying the FINZMOS territorial demand, but by granting it immediately, before the communities could put minimal conditions in place for effective self-government.

Across the border in Nicaragua, we may well soon see what happens when a state follows this course of action. Out of power for sixteen years the Sandinista party, shorn of its overt socialist rhetoric, made pacts at every turn to ensure that the electoral arithmetic turned out right. An exceedingly contradictory coalition came to power in January 2007: part mobilization of the poor for relief from the pain of neoliberal development; part *comandante*-capitalists deeply invested – literally and ideologically – in this very model; part reassertion of the revolutionary mantle, with faint echoes of socialist idealism from days past, yet underwritten by the crass logic of political power at any cost. Among the many pacts that sealed the Sandinista victory was one with YATAMA, the powerful regional political party that represents Miskitu (and to a lesser extent other Costeños') interests. This pact was embodied in a remarkable document that grants nearly every important demand YATAMA had been struggling for over the past twenty-five years – with full and prompt recognition of territorial rights at front and centre.[24] President Daniel Ortega vigorously reaffirmed this commitment in an early March 2007 speech:

> our indigenous brothers and sisters ... live[d] in these territories from a time before the Nicaraguan state took shape; before the conquistadors arrived, they were there! They had their own nation, their people. They are the true owners of these lands, they are the original peoples ... we will respect the rights of Nicaragua's original peoples![25]

This assertion – that indigenous peoples were nations before the rise of the Nicaraguan state – was the shot across the bow that initiated an intense armed conflict with the Sandinistas twenty-five years ago. But, when the conflict began in 1981, territorial encompassment was the epitomizing principle of state rule; now the state has new reason to endorse selectively the principle of territorial decentralization. With Ortega leading the way, a World Bank-backed law on the books and an unprecedented presence of Costeño notables in high government positions, the conditions for achieving black and indigenous territorial rights are more propitious than ever before.

Yet one must assume that Ortega is open to territorial rights only to the extent that they do not interfere with the neoliberal development projects that the governing coalition also promotes in order to survive and prosper. In that same remarkable speech of March 2007, Ortega laid out his government's plans for economic development of the coastal region – African palm plantations, new roads, deep water ports and other mega-projects – a menu that sounds suspiciously like neoliberal business as usual. The profound uncertainty, indeed bordering on schizophrenia, of Nicaraguan national politics leaves the question of Atlantic coast land rights at a crossroads: between an expansive redrawing of the map that empowers multicommunal *bloques* and state-driven neoliberal development that treats community land rights as little more than a nuisance. Perhaps the most troubling scenario, however, is a volatile combination of these two, whereby the state allows, even celebrates, territorial autonomy, but only in the breach, that is, in the 'empty spaces' where neoliberal economic development has little appeal.

Garífuna activists from OFRANEH are on to this threat, and most inclined of the four organizations to confront it head on. The activist research dialogue with OFRANEH leaders yielded the mandate for a study similar to the one carried out with MASTA – cartography, legal research and ethnography – but under different conditions of political geography. Scattered along the northern Caribbean coast of Honduras, Garífuna communities are interspersed with private holdings by wealthy Hondurans and large-scale tourist development projects driven by transnational investment groups and fully backed by the Honduran state. Consistent with these conditions, the World Bank-financed Land Administration project (PATH) has promoted an individual community model of Garífuna land titling and OFRANEH has responded with a battery of

33

tactics – from street protest in the capital city to legal complaints with the Inter-American Human Rights Commission, to deft political manoeuvres designed to use the World Bank commitments to Afro-indigenous collective rights against the bank itself.[26] In all these struggles, the Iriona territory has been a crucial point of reference, as evidence for the legitimacy of the rights that the state and the development banks are violating. OFRANEH's tactics of radical refusal have been remarkably successful: putting the Honduran state on the defensive, exposing corruption and hypocrisy within the PATH, prompting the World Bank 'Inspection Panel' to visit Honduras to investigate OFRANEH complaints.[27] Yet the titling of the Iriona territory faces a series of truly daunting barriers. The Mestizo population settled within the territory is large and growing fast; its eastern boundary is mired in an intractable dispute with their Miskitu neighbours;[28] the community members' plans for sustained economic betterment are still incipient, especially if they are to remain consistent with the collectivist ethos that drives the territorial claim. Indeed a principal mainstay of economic survival is remittances from the growing portion of community members who live outside the region. If OFRANEH's organizational prowess remains focused on a collective title to the Iriona territory, the *bloque* is likely to achieve some version of this claim. But the victory is bound to be partial and subject to limits; and management of the *bloque*'s political-economic affairs is sure to require unsavoury entanglements with the state at every turn.

Such entanglements make for a poor fit with OFRANEH's overall political style and strategy. These activists put forth a cogent and persuasive critique of the state and neoliberal capitalism, with a well-honed array of legal and political tactics that put this critique into action. They are fully capable of throwing a wrench in the gears to stop the machine, which in turn creates a little more room for the next manoeuvre. Yet they have little stomach for compromise with the neoliberal state and reserve a sharp critique for those who succumb to the governmental effects that inevitably follow. Onto the menace of neoliberal subject formation, they respond by assuming the role of the impossible subject: analytically acute; willing to talk but only according to their own rules; preferring continued protest over incomplete concessions; always a force to contend with, in large part because they are so difficult to pin down. The high-stakes perpetual mobilization of the impossible subject is surely the most effective defence against this form of neoliberal governance, but it comes with a difficult bargain: elude the entanglements, but forgo the quite significant benefits as well.

Reflections

These four land rights struggles face a strategic predicament: how to occupy the spaces opened for indigenous and black land rights in Central America, without being overwhelmed by their governance effects? On the one hand, these spaces are profoundly contaminated. The 'structural break' in the regional political-economy has relegated large portions of what black and indigenous peoples claim to the economic periphery, therefore rendering them symbolically empty. The neoliberal state is divesting itself of its mandate for territorial encompassment, opting instead for differentiated zones of govern-ance fashioned according to entrepreneurial criteria.[29] These developments are largely compatible with the partial recognition of cultural rights and with limited notions of territorial autonomy as well. Generous funding from multilateral institutions such as the World Bank drives and reinforces these transformations, breathing life into government dispositions that otherwise would be likely to remain as underfunded mandates and empty rhetoric. Under these conditions, rather than a high-stakes battle to fend off the neoliberal threat, the struggle for land rights runs the risk of complicity with neoliberal governance: meeting with success according to circumscribed patterns, in keeping with rules set in advance. On the other hand, organizations that avoid these entanglements through radical refusal often have trouble meeting their members' immediate material needs and risk forgoing the substantial benefits that the territorial turn entails. The predicament, in sum, rests on the premise that these two modes of struggle – one immediate and pragmatic, the other expansive with sights set on the horizon – are incompatible.

A parallel problem runs through recent theoretical dialogues around the notion of resistance. Over the past two decades we have received a steady flow of cautionary notes, expressing a healthy scepticism about celebratory or overly dichotomous approaches to the topic. James C. Scott (1990) objected to the premises embedded in theoretical approaches inspired by Gramsci, alleging that they tied the notion of resistance too closely to a predetermined path of structural transformation; he directed us instead to appreciate the everyday resistance, often hidden and off-stage, expressed in oppressed people's constant, quiet efforts to get by and get ahead.[30] Lila Abu-Lughod's memor-able phrase 'romance of resistance' admonished us to avoid inflicting our own search for radical subjects onto the people we study, and redirected our analytical efforts from resistance to a diagnosis of how power is exercised (Abu-Lughod, 1990; see also Ortner, 1995; Brown, 1996). In keeping with this mandate, Foucault-inflected ethnography ushered in ever greater sophistica-tion, helping us to appreciate the dispersed heterogeneity of power relations, focusing attention on subject formation, replacing the broad dichotomy between domination and resistance with more nuanced appreciations of fluidity, ambiguity, internal fissures and contradictions. Using a Foucauldian interpretative lens, close ethnographic scrutiny could always uncover yet another irony, twist and turn in the narrative or unintended consequence that justifies seasoned scepticism of the activist's passionate clarity. But these two correctives – salutary as they may be – have left us at an impasse: proponents of 'everyday resistance' end up finding resistance everywhere and lose the ability to think incisively about strategies for social transformation;

deconstruction runs the risk of the scholar's conceit, a discursive radicalism that critiques power at every turn, but in perpetual deferral of the political cut.

Activist research can help to invigorate this dialogue, generating insight into the theoretical impasse through direct engagement with the corresponding on-the-ground predicament. This is no absence of an expansive, even utopian horizon in these land rights struggles. Whether framed in the more universalist language of the world social forum or in place-specific allusions to territorial dominion, racial empowerment or cultural ascendancy, the protagonists regularly conjure broader political visions for their movements. To dismiss these visions as overly dichotomous or essentialist would be to overlook their resonance and vitality for many of those directly involved. The central problem comes, rather, in fashioning a path for moving effectively towards distant political horizons. What could well appear as manageable tactical differences – between occupying limited spaces and holding out for more – often turn deeply ideological, because neoliberal governance feeds on the common-sense assertion that these limited spaces are all that any reasonable person could hope to achieve. The impossible subject is onto this threat and responds by refusing to engage, thereby keeping a transformative notion of resistance alive, but running the risk of leaving immediate needs unmet and failing to offer a bridge between utopian horizons and the material here and now. In the response to this dilemma we need to reframe resistance as the art of articulation, between everyday and transformative struggles, between the insistence on occupying limited spaces and the adamant refusal of the premises on which those spaces are predicated.

The activist research on land rights that we have carried out over the past decade has been a series of experiments with precisely such efforts of articulation. Our research NGO – known by the acronym CCARC – competed for and won the two World Bank-funded diagnostic studies, in Nicaragua (1996–7) and Honduras (2001–2), referred to earlier in this article.[31] However dubious this tactic appeared, we reasoned that using participatory mapping methods and working in close collaboration with our black and indigenous organizational allies, we could occupy the space opened by the commissioned research and help to articulate the results with the rising tide of black and indigenous mobilization for territorial rights, against the neoliberal onslaught. The vindication of this wager was to be achieved through the subsequent efforts described in greater detail here. Working directly with the same organizations, now freed from the constraints of World Bank-funded research, we expected to accompany those who were bringing a selection of these claims to fruition, contributing to a major frontal challenge to the neoliberal state and to a measure of political empowerment based on territorial rights. Ironically, we found that the chances of gaining at least some significant portion of these territorial rights have grown, while the prospects that these rights would pose a frontal challenge to neoliberal governance have diminished.

My conclusion is not that the original wager has been lost, but, rather, that the articulating principle needs to be recalibrated. As the state shifts emphasis from a territorial to an entrepreneurial logic, and neoliberal economic development envelops – albeit unevenly – the entire space in contention, demands for autonomy as previously conceived can no longer serve as the horizon for transformative politics. The struggle for rights to land and resources retains a compelling rationale, as symbolic justice, a means to achieve modest improvements in community livelihood and a stronger base from which to confront future threats and seize opportunities. But the notion of autonomy, understood as negotiated devolution of authority from state to a given enclosed space, has come to fit too comfortably within the repertoire of the neoliberal state to serve also as these movements' political horizon. Rather than capitulation to the limited technical fix that neoliberalism prescribes, we need a recalibrated principle of articulation: a means to connect the here-and-now of communal and multicommunal land rights struggles with a more expansive answer to Marta's lingering question, *'resistencia para que?'*

The most promising line of analysis that has emerged from our participatory mapping research thus far focuses on a revised notion of autonomy, grounded in a more circumspect stance towards territorial rights. The new emphasis is less on improving the terms of devolution of authority from the state to autonomous unit and more on reducing these ties of dependency and tutelage altogether. It is less about incrementally improving the terms of economic relations and more about finding ways to achieve an ever increasing measure of self-sustaining production. In regard to political horizons, this radicalized notion of autonomy is adamantly local, but also potentially more transnational in scope. At a meeting of the land rights project not long ago, Marta and her counterpart activist intellectuals from Nicaragua and Guatemala took a moment to sketch this image: contiguous territories controlled by black and indigenous communities, connecting the 'empty spaces', forging transnational connections to counteract the debilitating influence of internal negotiations with their respective states. This is an inspiring image, even if it leaves open a number of very difficult questions: how to engage the global economy? How to avoid the straitjacket of rights tied to particular cultural identities, bounded in a particular geographic space? On what terms can race- and culture-based mobilizations for rights reconnect with the political aspirations of their Mestizo counterparts? What to do about the state? These are the questions that the resurgent leftist movements of our times must confront.

My more specific burden here has been to convey the key findings of this research in the form of significant advances in social science knowledge about these struggles. I offer four points by way of conclusion. First, we are witnessing the gradual displacement of the territorial state in favour of its entrepreneurial successor, such that the fate of black and indigenous land claims has come to vary widely, depending on location in relation to the empty spaces or brown areas that neoliberal development has left behind.

My second point is to revise O'Donnell's description of the brown areas, making the case that the absence of the formal trappings of the territorial state does not necessarily preclude the workings of neoliberal governance. By granting land titles and local autonomy the state devolves limited rights and extensive responsibilities to the communities, which gain a resource base, but are fixed in place by a state-defined and regulated rights regime. Territorial rights bring new procedures, an endless flow of meetings, workshops and *capacitaciones*, modest employment possibilities for newly trained leaders, increased flows of outside aid, but they bring little means to challenge either the market-based discipline of the global economy or persisting state authority as ultimate arbiter of communities' political affairs.

This leads, third, to a predicament in the political strategies for these struggles in the neoliberal era: how to occupy the compromised spaces of cultural-political recognition, without losing sight of the utopian horizons that keep such efforts on track over the long haul? Finally, based on the experience of activist research, which grapples with that very predicament, my analysis highlights the need for a renewed principle of articulation, in the land rights struggles themselves and in our theoretical approaches to resistance. This principle can help move beyond the dichotomy between pragmatic notions of 'everyday' resistance and analysis that stops with the deconstruction of power relations; between the immediate material needs of these struggles and the expansive critical vision of the impossible subject. In the actual processes of struggle for land rights, these benefits often have been framed in terms of political heft: alliances, coalitions, unification of struggles in the face of the omnipresent threat of fragmentation. This forms part of my argument as well. But the central benefit comes, I contend, in the realm of collective political sensibilities: a potential to yield transformative dialogue, a democratic means to revision political strategies, among those who have starkly opposed responses to the neoliberal predicament. We might gauge the effects of neoliberal hegemony in our times by how awkward and out of place it feels to do this work of articulation, positioned adamantly on both sides of the chasm at once.

Acknowledgements

This paper has been presented in numerous places and has gone through a number of revisions to reach its current form. Here I gratefully acknowledge the venue and institutional sponsorship, without naming specific people involved: PRISMA, 2007 (San José, Costa Rica); AAA, 2007; University of Chicago, 2007; University of Oklahoma, 2007; University of Texas, 2008; and the Manchester workshop coordinated by Peter Wade. Special thanks to Edmund T. Gordon and other *compañeros/as* of CCARC for many long conversations, and the collective work that produced these ideas.

Notes

1   For Latin America-wide documentation of this transition, see Van Cott (2000) and Yashar (1998). Even Chile, perhaps the last holdout state in the multicultural turn, became a signatory to Convention 169 in 2008.

2   For some reflections on activist research methods (known by a variety of names), see Field (1999), Hale (2008), Lassiter (2005), Rappaport (2005) and Speed (2008).

3   The project involves multiple participants at each site. I am now at work on a monograph that explores these issues at much greater depth.

4   Fraternal Organization of Black Hondurans. For more information on historical and contemporary patterns of Garífuna organization, see Anderson (2000), Anderson and England (2004) and Euraque (2003).

5   This term was coined by Malkki (1995).

6   Consequently, Garífuna people's claims to rights based on indigenous culture and identity are constantly called into question, by state and multilateral actors, and even by some other indigenous leaders. See Anderson (2009).

7   This language conjures up an old, and much criticized distinction that Maxine Molyneaux once made between 'practical' and 'strategic' feminism (1986). I anticipate and accept the argument that 'pragmatic' politics can also be highly sophisticated and strategic. At the same time, I defend the basic observation that neoliberal ideology rewards pragmatism that is severed from critical analysis and broader political vision and vigorously discourages the articulation of the two.

8   Ample evidence for this state rhetoric and practice towards the coastal region can be found in Gordon (1998) and Hale (1994).

9   See Gupta and Ferguson (2002). For historical analysis of Central America that follows this line of argument, see various chapters in the volume edited by Dario Euraque, Jeffry Gould and Charlie Hale (2004).

10   Key sources here include Comisión para el Esclarecimiento Histórico (1999), Manz (2004) and Sanford (2003).

11   The best historical account of this period can be found in Barahona (2005).

12   The fine print of this decree allows foreigners to own beach land up to 3000 square metres and requires tourist investors first to acquire permission from the Ministry of Tourism. However, the decree opened the floodgates, beginning in the Caribbean island of Roatan (Stonich, 2000), and later spreading to the north coast. For some disturbing evidence of the latter, see the website, 'Real estate steals in Central America', http://www.dirla.com/honduras2_1b.htm (accessed 28 October 2008).

13   In writing this paragraph, I drew heavily on an unpublished report by Mark Anderson, completed in the year 2000, carried out as part of a study of black and indigenous organization in Central America.

14   The PATH project, approved in February 2004 and initiated in December 2004, was a 25 million dollar loan designed to build on the purported success of a antecedent project, called PAAR, which had similar objectives and counted among its achievements the titling of thirteen Tolupán indigenous community lands. Ample background information can be found in the online documents associated with the OFRANEH claim against the World Bank, which set in motion a full-fledged investigation of the Bank Inspection Panel: http://www-wds.worldbank.org/external/default/WDS ContentServer/WDSP/IB/2006/03/20/000160016_20060320124837/Rendered/ PDF/35470.pdf (accessed 28October 2008). The Property Law (Ley de Propiedad Decreto No. 82/2004) became effective on 29 June 2004.

15   There is an active debate as to whether promoting these marginal enterprises could be a pro-poor development strategy. One telling test case will be Tela Bay in Honduras, where Garífuna-controlled community tourist enterprises exist on the perimeter of a vast mega-tourist development project.

16   For a Latin America-wide analysis of this problem, see Godoy (2005).

17   This is nicely documented in a detailed article authored by David Kaimowitz (2002).

18   Two articles of this law, #94 and #100, affirm the right of blocs of communities to claim their land, in accordance with 'traditional forms of tenancy and communal property', and recognize these community properties as inalienable. However, in other articles of the same law, conditions are introduced that leave the efficacy of the rights in question. As of this writing, the law had yet been put to the test.

19   Some facets of this same logic apply to Afro-descendant peoples, but not all. Anderson (2007), Hooker (2005) and Ng'weno (2007) among others have given this slippage scholarly attention.

20   This last effect, which I have conceived as the construction of the space of the 'indio permitido' is worked out in Hale (2004, 2006b).

21   For ethnographic evidence along these lines, see Hale (2005).

22   I am thinking especially of the collectively researched historical study coordinated by Arturo Taracena (2002).

23   This problem is analysed at great length in Velasquez Nimatuj (2005).

24   Text in the author's possession.

25   Text in the author's possession.

26   As one OFRANEH leader explained this series of manoeuvres, 'we are using the system against the system' (quoted in Hale, 2006a, pp. 111–12).

27   The Inspection Panel report, which includes full documentation of the complaint and the Panel's judgment, is dated 14 March 2006 and posted at: http://www-wds.world bank.org/servlet/main?menuPK=64187510&pagePK=64193027&piPK=64187937 &theSitePK=523679&entityID=000160016_20060320124837 (accessed 29 October 2008).

28   For useful background on the border conflict, see Mollett (2006).

29   Aihwa Ong (2006) has referred to this reconfiguration as 'graduated zones of sovereignty'.

30   Scott (1990) even suggests that these small acts are what, cumulatively, make the most difference in the long run.

31   This first of these is described in Gordon et al. (2003).

References

Abu-Lughod, L. (1990). *The romance of resistance*: Tracing transformations of power through Bedouin women. *American Ethnologist*, *17*(1), 41–55.

Anaya, S. J. & Grossman, C. (2002). The case of Awas Tingni v. Nicaragua: A new step in the international law of indigenous peoples. *Arizona Journal of International and Comparative Law*, *19*(1), 1–15.

Andersen, M. E. (2006). Failing states, ungoverned spaces and the indigenous challenge in Latin America. Retrieved 29 October 2008 from http://www.ndu. edu/chds/journal/PDF/2006/ Andersen_essay–formatted.pdf

Anderson, M. (2000). Garifuna kids: Blackness, modernity and tradition in Honduras. Dissertation, University of Texas.

Anderson, M. (2007). When Afro becomes (like) indigenous: Garifuna and Afro–indigenous politics in Honduras. *Journal of Latin American and Caribbean Anthropology*, *12*(2), 384–413.

Anderson, M. (2009). *Black and Indigenous: Garifuna activism and consumer culture in Honduras*. Minneapolis: University of Minnesota Press.

Anderson, M. & England, S. (2004). ¿Auténtica cultura Africana en Honduras? Los afro-centroamericanos desafían el

mestizaje indo-hispánico hondureño. In
C. R. Hale, J. Gould & D. Euraque (Eds.),
*Memorias del mestizaje: Cultura política en
Centroamérica 1920–presente*. Antigua,
Guatemala: CIRMA.
Anderson, P. (2000). Renewals. *New Left
Review 1*(January–February).
Barahona, M. (2005). *Honduras en el siglo
XX: Una sintesis historica*. Tegucigalpa:
Editorial Guaymuras.
Brown, M. F. (1996). On resisting
resistance. *American Anthropologist, 98*(4),
729–34.
Bryan, J. (2007). Map or be mapped:
Land, race, and property in eastern
Nicaragua. Dissertation, University of
California, Berkeley.
Comisión para el Esclarecimiento
Histórico. (1999). *Las violaciones de los
derechos humanos y los hechos de violencia*
(Vol. 3). Guatemala: UNOPS.
Euraque, D. (1998). The banana enclave,
nationalism, and mestizaje in Honduras,
1910s–1930s. In A. Chomsky &
A. Lauria-Santiago (Eds.), *Identity and
struggle at the margins of the nation-state:
The laboring peoples of Central America and
the Hispanic Caribbean* (pp. 151–68).
Durham, NC: Duke University Press.
Euraque, D. (2003). The threat of
blackness to the nation: Race and ethnicity
in the banana economy, 1920s and 1930s.
In S. Striffler & M. Moberg (Eds.),
Banana wars (pp. 229–52). Durham, NC:
Duke University Press.
Euraque, D., Gould, J. & Hale, C. R.
(Eds.) (2004). *Memorias del mestizaje:
Cultura y política en Centroamérica, 1920 al
presente*. Guatemala: CIRMA/Cholsamaj.
Ferguson, J. (2006). *Global shadows:
Africa in the neoliberal world order*.
Durham, NC: Duke University Press.
Field, L. W. (1999). Complicities and
collaborations: Anthropologists and the
'unacknowledged tribes' of California.
Current Anthropology, 40(2), 193–209.
Gill, L. (2000). *Teetering on the rim:
Global restructuring, daily life, and the
armed retreat of the Bolivian state*.
New York: Columbia University Press.
Godoy, A. S. (2005). *Popular injustice:
Violence, community, and law in Latin
America*. Stanford, CA: Stanford
University Press.

Goett, J. (2006). Diasporic identities,
autochthonous rights: Race, gender, and
the cultural politics of Creole land rights
in Nicaragua. Dissertation, University of
Texas.
Gonzalez, M. (2008). Governing multi-
ethnic societies in Latin America:
Regional autonomy, democracy, and the
state in Nicaragua 1987–2007.
Dissertation, York University.
Gordon, E. T. (1998). *Disparate diasporas:
Identity and politics in an African-
Nicaraguan community*. Austin: University
of Texas Press.
Gordon, E. T., Gurdian, G. C. & Hale,
C. R. (2003). Rights, resources and the
social memory of struggle: Reflections on
a study of indigenous and black
community land rights on Nicaragua's
Atlantic coast. *Human Organization, 62*(4),
369–81.
Gros, C. (n.d.). ¿Territorios
multiculturales? Unpublished paper.
Gupta, A. & Ferguson, J. (2002).
Spacializing states. *American Ethnologist,
29*(4), 981–1003.
Hale, C. R. (1994). *Resistance and
contradiction: Miskitu Indians and the
Nicaraguan state, 1894–1987*. Stanford,
CA: Stanford University Press.
Hale, C. R. (2002). Does
multiculturalism menace? Governance,
cultural rights and the politics of identity
in Guatemala. *Journal of Latin American
Studies, 34*, 485–524.
Hale, C. R. (2004). Rethinking
Indigenous politics in the era of the 'indio
permitido'. *NACLA, 38*(1), 16–20.
Hale, C. R. (2005). Neoliberal
multiculturalism: The remaking of
cultural rights and racial dominance in
Central America. *Polar, 28*(1), 10–28.
Hale, C. R. (2006a). Activist research v.
cultural critique: Indigenous land rights
and the contradictions of politically
engaged anthropology. *Cultural
Anthropology, 21*(1), 96–120.
Hale, C. R. (2006b). 'Más que un
indio . . .': Racial ambivalence and
neoliberal multiculturalism in Guatemala*.
Santa Fe, NM: School of American
Research Press.
Hale, C. R. (Ed.) (2008). *Engaging
contradictions: Theory, politics and methods*

of activist scholarship. Berkeley: University of California Press.

Hale, C. R. & Millaman, R. (2006). Cultural agency and political struggle in the era of the 'indio permitido'. In D. Sommer (Ed.), *Cultural agency in the Americas* (pp. 281–304). Durham, NC: Duke University Press.

Hooker, J. (2005). Indigenous inclusion/black exclusion: Race, ethnicity and multicultural citizenship in Latin America. *Journal of Latin American Studies, 37,* 1–26.

Hurtado Paz y Paz, L. (2008). *Dinámicas agrarias y reproducción campesina en la globalización: El caso de Alta Verapaz, 1970–2007.* Guatemala: F&G Editores.

Kaimowitz, D. (2002). Resources, abundance and competition in the Bosawas Biosphere Reserve, Nicaragua. In R. Matthew, M. Halle & J. Switzer (Eds.), *Conserving the peace: Resources, livelihoods and security.* Winnipeg, MB: International Institute for Sustainable Development.

Lassiter, L. E. (2005). Collaborative ethnography and public anthropology. *Current Anthropology, 46*(1), 83–106.

Macleod Howland, M. (1997). *Poder local: Reflexiones sobre Guatemala.* Guatemala: OXFAM.

Malkki, L. H. (1995). *Purity and exile: Violence, memory, and national cosmology among Hutu refugees in Tanzania.* Chicago, IL: University of Chicago Press.

Manz, B. (2004). *Paradise in ashes: A Guatemalan journey of courage, terror, and hope.* Berkeley: University of California Press.

Mollett, S. (2006). Race and natural resource conflicts in Honduras: The Miskito and Garifuna struggle for Lasa Pulan. *Latin American Research Review, 41*(1), 76–101.

Molyneux, M. (1986). Mobilization without emancipation? Women's interests, state, and revolution. In R. Fagen, C. D Deere & J. L Coraggio (Eds.), *Transition and development problems of Third World socialism.* New York: Monthly Review Press.

Ng'weno, B. (2007). *Turf wars: Territory and citizenship in the contemporary state.* Stanford, CA: Stanford University Press.

O'Donnell, G. (1999). *Counterpoints: Selected essays on authoritarianism and democratization.* Notre Dame, IN: University of Notre Dame Press.

Offen, K. H. (2003). The territorial turn: Making black territories in Pacific Colombia. *Journal of Latin American Geography, 2*(1), 43–73.

Ong, A. (2006). *Neoliberalism as exception. Mutations in citizenship and sovereignty.* Durham, NC: Duke University Press.

Ortner, S. (1995). Resistance and the Problem of ethnographic refusal. *Comparative Studies in Society and History, 37*(1), 173–93.

Padilla, G. *et al.* (2007). Informe final de investigacion. CCARC.

Postero, N. (2007). *Now we are citizens: Indigenous politics in post-multicultural Bolivia.* Stanford, CA: Stanford University Press.

Programa de Apoyo a la Integración Regional Centroamericana. (2003). Diagnóstico integral sobre las principales tendencias de las relaciones económicas intraregionales y de las necesidades de formación de los actores identificados. Retrieved from http://www.sica.int/busqueda/Centro%20de%20Documentación.aspx?IDItem=9646&IdCat=12&IdEnt=55&Idm=1&IdmStyle=1

Rappaport, J. (2005). *Intercultural utopias: Public intellectuals, cultural experimentation, and ethnic pluralism in Colombia.* Durham, NC: Duke University Press.

Rivera Cusicanqui, S. (2004). Reclaiming the nation. *NACLA, 39*(3), 19–23.

Roldan, R. (2005). Importancia de los territorios colectivos de indigenas y afroamericanos en el desarrollo rural. In R.G. Echeverria (Ed.), *Desarrollo territorial rural en América Latina y el Caribe: Manejo sostenible de recursos naturales, acceso a tierras y finanzas rurales* (pp. 135–61). Washington, DC: Inter-American Development Bank.

Sanford, V. (2003). *Buried secrets.* New York: Palgrave.

Scott, J. C. (1990). *Domination and the arts of resistance: Hidden transcripts.* New Haven, CT: Yale.

Segovia, A. (2005). *Integración real y grupos de poder económico en América Central: Implicaciones para la democracia y el desarrollo de la región.* San Jose, Costa Rica: Fundacion Friedrich Ebert.

Speed, S. (2008). *Rights in rebellion: Indigenous struggle and human rights in Chiapas.* Stanford, CA: Stanford University Press.

Stonich, S. C. (2000). *The other side of paradise: Tourism, conservation, and development in the Bay Islands.* New York: Cognizant Communication Corporation.

Taracena Arriola, A. (2002). *Etnicidad, estado y nación en Guatemala, 1808–1944.* Guatemala: Nawal Wuj.

Van Cott, D. L. (2000). *The friendly liquidation of the past: The politics of diversity in Latin America.* Pittsburgh, PA: University of Pittsburgh Press.

Velasquez Nimatuj, I. A. (2005). Indigenous peoples, the state and struggles for land in Guatemala: Strategies for survival and negotiation in the face of globalized inequality. PhD dissertation, University of Texas at Austin.

Yashar, D. (1998). Contesting citizenship: Indigenous movements and democracy in Latin America. *Comparative Politics, 31*(1), 23–42.

Localized neoliberalism, multiculturalism and global religion: exploring the agency of migrants and city boosters

Nina Glick Schiller

Abstract

This paper examines the discourse on citizenship and cultural values in Manchester, New Hampshire, USA, a city that has received many immigrants. The author examines how multiculturalism was endorsed by political and economic city leaders in their initial efforts to reinvent their city within an agenda of neoliberal re-structuring, but rejected generally by the very migrants deemed to embody cultural difference. The migrants in the case study – from a wide array of countries – countered the push towards cultural politics with public *non-ethnic* identification with a global religion, Christianity, Buddhism or Islam. I suggest that in certain localities the universalistic claims of global religions have facilitated the local and transnational incorporation of migrants in ways that reject aspects of both multi-culturalism and neoliberalism.

Building on Charles Hale's concept of 'neoliberal multiculturalism', Susanne Brandtstädter, Peter Wade and Kath Woodward highlight systems of govern-ance that have sought to 'create self-organizing and self-regulating citizens' yet through 'multicultural politics "out-source" new forms of policing' and control to 'so-called "cultural communities"' (Brandtstädter et al., 2008). They argue that, despite the apparent philosophical disparity between neoliberalism's focus on individualism and multiculturalism's promotion of communities of cultural difference, the two regimes have in specific instances come together within a single system of governance. Their interest is in how the power to socially construct identifiers of radical difference in itself obscures the relationship of unequal power. Brandtstädter, Wade and Woodward (2008) note that 'if "culture" becomes the field through which to voice a political radicalism, any political challenge can be either easily deflected as "fundamentalist," "traditional" or "backward" (that is, as illiberal) or defined as a problem that must be solved "internally" (that is, by the community itself)'. That is, while multicultural liberalism has generated tensions, it also has created what I would call the hegemonic parameters of contemporary systems of governance (Hall, 1987; Williams, 1958). However, it is important to note that, while hegemonic agents – governmental, corporate or academic – continually construct narratives that define the parameters of debate and struggle, including forms of neoliberal multiculturalism, they are never completely successful because all social actors have multiple positionings from which to formulate identities and take actions (Hall, 1980 [1973]).

This article examines an instance in which multiculturalism was endorsed by political and economic city leaders in their initial efforts to reinvent their city within an agenda of neoliberal restructuring, but rejected generally by the very migrants deemed to embody cultural difference. The migrants in the case study – from a wide array of countries – countered the push towards cultural politics with public *non-ethnic* identification with a global religion, Christianity, Buddhism or Islam. I suggest that in certain localities the universalistic claims of global religions have facilitated the local and transnational incorporation of migrants in ways that reject aspects of both multiculturalism and neoliberalism. By universalistic I refer to a belief system that claims to apply to all people, governments, places and times. At the same time, the case study provides insights into the ways in which migrants may use the domains of opportunity opened to them by neoliberal restructuring to build pathways of local and transnational incorporation. Neoliberalism can provide ways to resist multicultural othering but, as I indicate in the conclusion, the incorporative opportunities it offers migrants may prove to be ephemeral.

The article contains a further rumination and cautionary note about theorizing the relationship about neoliberal governance and multiculturalism: the need to address the positioning of a specific locality within neoliberal rescaling processes. In cities that lose out in restructuring efforts, migrants may develop non-ethnic forms of life worlds, contestatory identities and social capital based on local and transnational incorporation. These alternatives to multiculturalism may be pathways to local incorporation and transnational connection that are significant both to migrants and the cities in which they live. Such alternative incorporations may in the short term lead migrants to practise and endorse neoliberal practices, but also to challenge values that accompany and legitimate neoliberal transformations.

To make these arguments, I examine the response of migrants to neoliberal multiculturalism in Manchester, New Hampshire, USA. Manchester is a city that has had difficulty in gaining sufficient access to the economic, political or cultural flows of national and global capital that are necessary for building the 'new economies' of neoliberal restructuring. Offering a locally specific approach to globally circulating narratives of multiculturalism and neoliberalism, I examine their implementation as a mode of governance, and how they work in relation to migrants' terms of engagement within a down-scaled city such as Manchester. The term 'down-scaled city' refers to a city that as a result of rescaling processes has relatively little political, economic or cultural importance globally, nationally or regionally, although as is the case of most cities today, it has been transformed by global connections and the implementation of a neoliberal agenda (Glick Schiller & Çağlar, 2009).

In down-scaled Manchester, migrants built non-ethnic religious affiliations, practices and identities, in conjunction with other forms of non-ethnic networks, as a means of local and global incorporation. In this way, they challenged the multiculturalist discourse and its regime of governance, including the right of the nation-state to allocate citizenship. It is important to note that, while migrants in Manchester utilized non-ethnic Muslim, Buddhist and Christian pathways of local and transnational incorporation, fundamentalist Christian networks were the most effective in definitively challenging multiculturalism, while facilitating migrants' entrance into opportunities facilitated by neoliberal restructuring and its governance regime (Glick Schiller, 2005). To the extent that they invoked neo-conservative rather than neoliberal values of family, collectivity, age and gender hierarchy, these migrants also challenged the current legitimation of neoliberal individuality and consumerism, but not the underlying globe-spanning institutional structure or hierarchy of power of capital.

Neoliberalism, multiculturalism and locality

A grounded analysis of the intersection of neoliberalism and multiculturalism is needed in order to understand how migrants' local and transnational incorporations are both shaped by and are part of urban restructuring and re-scaling. Based on this case study and other ethnographic accounts of the relationship between neoliberal restructuring and re-scaling of cities and pathways of migrant incorporation, I suggest that various intersections of neoliberal and multicultural narratives and their accompanying policy implementations and practices must be examined through the lens of locality (Glick Schiller & Çağlar, 2009, 2011; Glick Schiller *et al.*, 2006). Neoliberalism can be defined as a series of contemporary projects of capital accumulation that, beginning in the 1970s, sought to reconstitute social relations of production, including the organization of labour, space, state institutions, military power, governance, membership and sovereignty (Harvey, 2005, 2006; Jessop, 2002). Neoliberalism has facilitated the creation of wealth, by destroying and replacing previous relations of production, consumption and distribution, and the generation of new forms of desire. That is to say: neoliberal agendas have been new instantiations of more general processes of capital accumulation that are characterized by Marx as 'creative destruction'.

The term 'agenda' is useful because neoliberal projects have taken the form of specific sets of ideas and policies instituted in various geographic scales of city, state and region that may or may not be successfully implemented. These projects involved not just the domain of economics, but also politics, cultural practices, ideas about self and society, and the production and dissemination of images and narratives. These have been localized through what can be termed neoliberal restructuring, a summary concept used to describe efforts to reorganize institutions, ownership, governance and senses of self. When applied to cities, the purpose of this reorganization has been to attract and facilitate flows of capital, new economy industry, tourists and skilled labour within the global economy (Brenner & Theodore, 2002; Marcuse & van Kempen, 2000).

It is important to situate actual existing multiculturalism within national as well as local projects of restructuring. While critics of multicultural discourse, whether they have been politicians or scholars, have centred their fears of immigrant 'difference' around the question of loyalty (Baber, 2008; Davis, 2005; Huntington, 1996), in point of fact multiculturalism 'does not question the territory principal' and 'maintains the idea of a primary belonging to one society and a loyalty to just one nation-state' (Castles & Davidson, 2000, p. 5). For this reason, each nation-state has had its own variant of multiculturalism and its form of reaction against it, although specific national backlashes have at the same time been part of a broader globally circulating discourse of blaming foreigners for the growing disparities, inequalities and displacement brought by neoliberal restructuring (Brubaker, 2001).

The critics of a multiculturalist ideology have chosen to ignore the fact that actual existing multiculturalism has generally been encompassed within specific nation-state building projects. Public policies as well as advocates of multiculturalism in specific countries have sought to use multicultural representations to facilitate the integration of newcomers by ensuring that they identify with their new country and build a cultural identity within it (Modood, 2007; Parekh, 2000; Takaki, 1993). Or, in the words of the police chief of Manchester New Hampshire: 'It's fine if immigrants celebrate their roots and keep their identities and national flags as long as the flag at the top of the flagpole is American' (Glick Schiller, field notes, 2002).

If the junctures between multiculturalism and neoliberalism must be analysed within the mutual imbrication of the local, national and global, they must also be analysed in time. As the 1990s proceeded, basic tensions within the neoliberal narrative of increasing prosperity through an unregulated global free market emerged. Neoliberal restructuring and structural adjustment led to the deterioration of the living conditions of both the impoverished populations and sectors of the middle classes all around the world. At the same time, the abolition of a sense of the public and the development of a generation of individualistic consumers, divided into culturally differentiated markets and marketable identities, engendered a culture of nihilism (Sennett, 1998). Populations increasingly seemed to have little loyalty to, or solidarity with, the nation-states in which they lived. Yet nation-states were still providing the military, legal and economic institutions that underlay globe-spanning neoliberal agendas. Consequently, the challenge at the turn of the twenty-first century to those benefiting from the implementation of neoliberal agendas was to reinforce the nation-state as a unit of identification, even as national redistributive policies and regulation of institutions, finance capital, trade and taxation continued to be undermined. It is within this juncture that I situate the backlash against multiculturalism and the world-wide resurgence of nationalism and anti-immigrant rhetorics.

Been down so long: the struggle to re-brand

Between 2001 and 2005, I conducted ethnographic fieldwork and interviews together with a research team that included anthropologist Thad Guldbrandsen, as well as Peter Buchannan, a research assistant, and an array of students.[1] I continued to do participant observation and informal interviews in subsequent years. Most of the description about Manchester is based on ethnography in the form of participant observation in various meetings and public events and interviews with city leaders, business people and planners. Through these methods I obtained documents flyers, newspapers and pamphlets from which information about the city was gained. In Manchester, learning about the city is an ethnographic process because information about the city and political and economic processes is not centralized, while web sources are ephemeral and must be obtained in the course of the research.

We interviewed 115 migrants from Latin America, Africa, Asia and Europe, as well as officials, service providers and religious officials. We conducted on-going participant observation in Vietnamese, Bosnian, Congolese, Nigerian, Iraqi, Sudanese, Pakistani and Colombian households or workplaces. In addition, we also attended public meetings, religious services and events that concerned migrants.[2]

Although it is the largest city in the northern New England region of the United States, Manchester, with a metropolitan region of approximately 210,000 inhabitants in 2005, was a struggling down-scale city for most of the twentieth century. In the nineteenth and early twentieth century Manchester claimed to have the largest textile mill in the world and its mills attracted a largely immigrant labour force. As had its namesake in England, Manchester's trade relations stretched around the world, although it was always subservient to Boston, located some 70 miles away, where the capitalists who owned the

Manchester mills continued to reside. During its period of intensive industrialization, Manchester had a large immigrant workforce with workers coming
from Quebec, as well as from a number of European countries (Hareven &
Langenbach, 1995). French Canadians and many other immigrant workers
were managed and disempowered through racialized stereotypes and other
forms of social exclusion. An official yearbook written during that period made
little or no mention of these populations, but photographs in this and other
official histories of the time portray a number of parades in the centre of the
city that included contingents of immigrant homeland associations; there is
also an image of city leaders feasting in a massive Chinese restaurant (Eastman,
1896). Beginning in the 1930s and continuing through the 1960s, Manchester
lost most of its textile industry and related industrial base. In the 1970s the
growth of suburban malls led to the demise of the central business and retail
district, just as a new wave of industrial downsizing and outsourcing led to the
closure of machine-tool shops that had remained viable in the region.

Since the 1980s, the local economy has been marked by a roller coaster of
expansion and subsequent contraction that has made it difficult for city leaders
to undertake a restructuring trajectory that can establish the city as a player
in the highly competitive post-industrial urban landscape. For example, in
the 1990s, the city in particular, and southern New Hampshire in general,
experienced a brief manufacturing effervescence as a result of broader rapid
neoliberal restructuring. The growth of hi-tech, defence and knowledge industries in the greater Boston area in the 1990s led to a demand for electronics and
other related products that could be obtained through a short supply chain.
This resulted in some investment, including direct foreign investment, in the
Manchester area in small non-union industrial factories that were part of complicated, flexible supply chains (Gittell, 2001). These small shops responded to
global competition by offering relatively low-cost production on the basis of
low-wage labour, much of it supplied by immigrants and refugees who began
to settle in the area. This period also saw new computer industries hiring
college-educated immigrants and the development of a local university that
attracted increasing numbers of foreign students who sought to settle in the
Manchester area and obtain work in these industries. In addition, Manchester
increasingly became a bedroom community for persons working in the belt of
hi-tech 'knowledge-oriented' industries that ringed Boston. For a short while,
the possibility that Manchester could be reinvented and restructured after its
long decline seemed bright.

However, the trajectory of growth could not be sustained. By the beginning
of the twenty-first century, in relationship to the US economic downturn of
2000 and the collapse of 'dot-com' investment and speculation, Manchester
factories once more began to close down. At this point, however, spurred by
the rising property values created by the demand for housing and services from
the new population influx, a section of Manchester's political and business
leaders began to reconfigure the city as a centre of financial and medical
services. They took these steps in the context of a global narrative of city

reinvention and branding. These efforts included the gentrification of the city centre, which was fuelled by public–private investment in buildings and infrastructure and in the sub-prime mortgage industry in the city's neighbourhoods. Manchester's new infrastructure included an entertainment arena complete with hockey team, a minor league baseball stadium and investment in the public schools, all supported by increased city taxes. Efforts were made to attract investment in the downtown city area with the development of high-rent high-rise housing, rehabilitated office buildings and a hotel complex that bordered the new ballpark. It was in the context of the new neoliberal boosterism that political and business leaders adopted a local narrative about the cultural diversity of Manchester. However, Manchester was unable to make a qualitative leap from its down-scaled positioning and the opportunity structure for both natives and migrants did not expand. The official unemployment rate, 2.4 per cent in 2000, had climbed to 4.3 per cent in 2004 (US Bureau of Labor Statistics, 2005).

Although there were no local statistics about migrant incorporation in the labour force, our interviews with migrants and local officials indicated that most immigrants continued to be employed in the shrinking number of industrial plants, while some obtained service industry jobs such as working with the disabled, sick and elderly. Many were employed below their educational levels, including those that had obtained higher education or retraining in New Hampshire. Migrants with poor English skills were unable to find sufficient service sector employment as office or hotel cleaners, restaurant workers or health care workers, as they might have done in global cities. The downtown development was not sufficient to provide adequate professional employment for educated natives or migrants.

The national and local politics of representation: from statist cultural pluralism to neoliberal multiculturalism

Multiculturalism is a public policy that highlights and validates ethnic organizational differentiation. In order to understand the links between multiculturalism and neoliberalism it is important to address the historical context of multiculturalism as an ideology and set of political practices and the varying outcome of efforts to institute multicultural policies at different times and in different places. Multiculturalism in the United States as an ideology of collective representation has a specific history and geographic setting that serves to illuminate its contemporary relationship to neoliberalism and its minimal success in down-scaled cities. Multiculturalism developed out of the cultural pluralist federal policies of the 1960s, which were used by the US federal government and powerful charitable institutions to counter and de-politicize the revolutionary politics of the black liberation movement (Basch et al., 1994; Glick Schiller et al., 1987). A programme that promised to 'empower' the urban poor through 'maximum feasible participation', which was initially pioneered by the Ford Foundation, was then implemented within a federal anti-poverty programme that funded local community groups organized along ethnic lines. In historic immigrant gateways, such as New York City, ethnic institutions and politics had actually always been part of local dynamics of power. Although the tripartite nature of the process is rarely acknowledged publicly, immigrant settlement in gateway cities in the United States generally has been a process of simultaneous cultural assimilation, ethnic organizational differentiation and transnational connection. At different times and in different places, one or another of these processes has been given prominence in public policy. In the 1960s, New York City institutions, long-imbued with the ethnic politics of the city, responded to the federal and charitable encouragement of displays of cultural diversity by further fostering ethnic community organizations and displays of ethnic identity.

In 1969, while researching the origins of institutionalized cultural pluralism, I had the opportunity to read all the post-Second World War flyers and directives sent by the New York City Board of Education to its public schools. I discovered a dramatic shift from a concern for Cold War civil defence preparation for nuclear war in the 1950s and early 1960s to a concentration, by 1968, on cultural pluralist school programmes. During the same period in New York, I found that the Southern Baptist Convention and the Catholic Diocese in the New York metropolitan area also began to value, celebrate and promote ethnic differences and ethnic organizing by immigrant groups. Most of the representations of culture in these ethnic organizations and in the public school programmes promoted a symbolic identity based on the celebration of ethnic roots, foods, flags, heroic figures and customs. For example, Haitian 'flag day', a Haitian national holiday, began to be celebrated in New York public schools that had large number of Haitian students. Research conducted by myself and Ida Susser in a New York City high school at the time indicated that students of migrant background, including Haitians, were encouraged to join a cultural club that celebrated the flag, holidays, dances and foods of their ancestral nationality.

Beginning in the 1970s, many US cities experienced various forms of neoliberal restructuring, which included disinvestment in public services and the de-industrialization and reconfiguration of urban space and employment. New York went into a fiscal crisis in 1975. In this context, while funding was reduced, support continued for forms of cultural representation that high-lighted national holidays, flags, song and dance. Social service organizations organized by and for specific ethnic groups remained prominent through the 1980s in gateway cities. Cultural pluralism was part of the institutional con-text within which new populations of immigrants and refugees settled in these cities and began to confront the local effects of neoliberal restructuring of the United States. New immigrants confronted de-industrialized cities, with pri-vatized social services and reduced federal housing and social programmes. To compete for the remaining funding, community activists in racialized migrant communities strengthened their claims to differentiated cultural citizenship, replacing the term 'cultural pluralism' with cultural citizenship and multi-culturalism and building on an emerging scholarship that highlighted and validated cultural difference (Benmayor *et al.*, 1992; Rosaldo, 1989). They spoke of the need to empower communities through bilingual programmes and through educators who were competent and aware of the culture of their students. This politics of cultural representation, which activists embraced as a way to counter the hegemonic Anglo-American narrative of American history and cultural heritage as well as obtain vital resources for migrant incorporation, soon became a gloss for the programmes that offered symbolic identities rather than addressed the growing disparities in wealth and power that accompanied neoliberal restructuring. By the 1990s, multiculturalism became one of the ways cities could rebrand themselves to attract international investment capital, global talent and hi-tech industries. New York City became a glittering city of consumption with its ethnic restaurants and neighbourhoods marketed as part of its cultural capital.

However, the institution of multiculturalist policies and their adoption by urban developers and promoters played out differently in cities that also had new migrants but were neither historic gateways nor successfully able to reinvent themselves within neoliberal trajectories. In the 1960s such cities received much less support from state intervention in the form of anti-poverty funding and fewer social agencies emerged. As forms of neoliberal governance in the form of decentralized funding and public-private partnerships emerged beginning in the 1970s, there was less of an economic or political base for the development of community-based multiculturalism. This was certainly true of Manchester, New Hampshire, where multiculturalist rhetoric and policies did not emerge until the beginning of the twenty-first century. When they did, multicultural narratives became part of a neoliberal form of urban redevelop-ment and boosterism, explicitly developed to accompany the restructuring of the city described above. It was at this point in the city's history that public officials and business people began to be trained in cultural competency and that celebrations of ethnic history and ethnic cuisines became publicly acknowledged as part of the political and cultural life of Manchester. It was believed by the city planners and councilmen I interviewed that a city needed to be seen as culturally diverse in order to attract sufficient private investment in new economy industries such as technology, finance and recreation.

Multiculturalism and neoliberal down-scaling

By the year 2000, despite the fact that new migrants were only about 4 per cent of the population, Manchester's city leaders on occasion began to foster celebrations of diversity and devoted public space to the promotion of the city's 'new diversity'. Officials and agencies began to speak of a new migration and of 'immigrant communities' in Manchester. Actually, migrants had never com-pletely stopped coming to the city, even after its decline as a manufacturing centre built on immigrant labour. Greeks arrived in the 1950s to work in the remaining mills and factories and Puerto Ricans fled the mean streets of Boston, New York or San Juan in the 1960s. Workers were recruited from Ecuador to work in local industry. The presence of Spanish-speaking migrants led to the establishment in 1972 of a Latin American centre that provided some services based on a mix of public funding and volunteer efforts.

However, in the 1990s a diverse migration of primary and secondary immigrants and refugees from all over the world began settling in the city. Refugee resettlement agencies identified Manchester as a location of affordable housing and available low-wage, low-skilled jobs. Refugees and immigrants also brought relatives directly from abroad to Manchester through US immigration laws that allow for marriage and family reunion. New refugees faced constraints on their freedom of choice, which made them into a docile workforce, a fact that attracted investors to the city. Refugees were forced to accept the first job offered to them or lose their entitlement to support from settlement agencies. Immigrants resettled in Manchester from Boston and New York, fleeing from crime, guns and drugs.

At the turn of the twenty-first century, during the height of multicultural politics in the US, the mayor of Manchester was Robert Baines, a populist Democrat who previously had been the head of the most prestigious of the city's three public high schools. The mayor embraced a public policy of multiculturalism, which he signalled at his inauguration ceremonies that began with immigrant children dressed in 'national costume' leading those assembled in the pledge of allegiance to the American flag. In his public speeches Mayor Baines explicitly linked Manchester's welcoming stance towards immigrants to the contribution they made to attracting and keeping factories in Manchester, as well as to Manchester's efforts to transform itself through gentrification and present a public image of a culturally diverse city. The city's new multiculturalist stance was also evident on the city's website, which in 2004 included a ten-minute video about Manchester that mentioned the multiplicity of the city's cultures several times. The video sought to attract both entrepreneurial capital and highly paid professionals to the city.

In Manchester, the celebration of difference in the city not only featured new immigrant identities, but also made salient the ethnic backgrounds of earlier waves of immigrants whose cultural presence had received little public acknowledgement in past decades. For example, the city welcomed a St Patrick's Day Parade and Greek Glendi, African-Caribbean and Latino festivals. A Cultural Diversity Task Force circulated a monthly newsletter that noted the holidays of various ethnic groups in the city, although in many cases migrants from these groups had little or no formal organization in the city.

On the surface the public celebration of multiculturalism seemed to reflect an effervescence of ethnic community organizing. During the five years of our research we contacted organizations, many of them newly formed, that represented ethnic and pan-ethnic groups including Haitian, Mexican, Vietnamese, Congolese, African, Hispanic, Indian and African-American/Caribbean.

However, few of these organizations had constituencies that extended beyond their leadership or offered assistance in settling or other social services. Only the Latin American centre, established much earlier, received any consistent public funding and by the end of our fieldwork it was on its last legs.

The globe-spanning narrative of prosperity through the promotion of private wealth accumulation at the beginning of the twenty-first century resonated throughout New Hampshire, which has a long history of anti-tax sentiment and an entrenched critique of public investment in social services. Moreover, in the new neoliberal 'geographies of governance', in which national policies have reduced the distribution of funds for urban redevelopment and placed cities under increasing pressure to attract transnational flows of capital, Manchester faced reduced access to public monies and resources (Peck, 1998). The city had a shrinking industrial tax base and new commitments to infrastructure projects but little money for city services and little or no money for services for migrants. Unlike globally powerful cities, such as New York, very few public or private agencies provided migrants with opportunities to develop careers as culture brokers who could represent the needs or interests of particular ethnicities. Also, unlike New York City, the newly formed ethnic organizations in Manchester lacked the skills, professionalized personae or organization to document their ability to function as a profit-making 'self-sufficient' business, a requirement of the neoliberal understanding of 'community' organizations. Moreover, they lacked the political clout to obtain federal grants that encouraged the conversion of local organizations into the new business model and they did not have the networks and professionalism to attract local charitable sources.[3]

Despite their efforts at city banding and promotion though occasional public celebrations of diversity using a narrative that had become the benchmark of neoliberal visions of urban redevelopment, Manchester officials and developers had little to offer migrant organizations or any sector of the migrant population. Multiculturalist rhetoric was not accompanied by public or charitable investment in organizations led by migrants or focused on developing ethnic pride or cultural diversity. Instead, the very little public and charitable funding was generally made available to a population defined in terms of a 'special need', rather than on the basis of cultural difference. In Manchester, there were services for the poor, the homeless, people with AIDS, severely disabled children and persons defined by the general category of 'minority' rather than by specific cultural heritage.

Those persons of migrant background who were able to achieve political or public prominence did so, not as ethnic leaders, but on the basis of party politics that build local non-ethnic constituencies. If their foreignness has been at all publicly marked, it was on occasions when they played the role of what I call a *public foreigner* – a person called on to be general representative of and spokesperson for foreigners in the city, rather than a representative of a particular ethnic group. In short, while Manchester occasionally flaunted multiculturalisms as part of the public representation of the urban environment, unlike in gateway cities such as New York, there was little viable ethnic organizing and ethnic community organizations received almost no public or charitable support.

In terms of their position on migration, Manchester political and corporate leaders and the urban developers with whom they worked were pulled in different directions by competing sets of interests. City leaders understood multicultural celebrations of diversity as a part of creating an urban lifestyle that would attract investors and the 'creative classes' whose presence was felt necessary to gentrify and reinvent the city (Florida, 2002). For example, the local Chamber of Commerce continued to claim that: '[t]oday the city of Manchester remains a diverse melting pot. Its diversity is demonstrated in the number of languages spoken at home by Manchester school children which currently tops 70' (Greater Manchester Chamber of Commerce, 2009). Yet city leaders also understood immigrants and refugees as a burden on local public and social services, which came under increasing pressure as federal monies receded and tax monies were channelled into public-private partnerships to develop entertainment, hotels and office complexes. The very same statistics of linguistic diversity in the schools were also used to substantiate the claim that migrants imposed excessive demands on city services, especially on public schools and the police.

Even the public celebration of ethnic diversity as a desirable part of gentrification held elements of racialization, commodification and objectification that were far from welcoming. Many of these mixed messages are concentrated in an article entitled 'Multicultural Manchester: The changing faces of the queen city', in *Hippo*, a free newspaper, marketed to a youthful readership that identifies with a new gentrified Manchester (Stewart, 2006). In a short space, and even as he is lauding the merits of multicultural Manchester, the author manages to equate cultural difference with physical appearance (beginning with the double meanings of the article's headline), ignore the previous racialization of French Canadians, erase the Hispanic migration of the 1960s and blame the 'diverse' newcomers for strains on city resources.

For most of its history, Manchester, like the rest of New Hampshire, has been lily-white in its make-up. Even the immigrants have been white: French Canadian, Irish, Bosnian, Dutch. For a long time, the concept of a minority population was scarcely more than that – even a wild idea. Minorities – people of color – were in the South or in New York, or Boston, but not here in the Great White North. Even as the rest of the United States became the world's melting pot, the Queen City remained racially unmixed. The minority population here at one time, it is said, was a guy named Eddie. But my, how our hue is changing. These days it's not uncommon to see women in kaftans in the Mall of New Hampshire or men in turbans driving down Elm Street – definitely not your traditional New Englanders. From all over the world, people of color are making their homes in the Queen City and the rest of Hillsborough

County. And they're bringing their languages, cultures and cuisines along with them. . . .

For all of the challenges posed by an increasing number of immigrants and refugees making their homes in Manchester, and the strain put upon local resources – from the health department to the school district – nearly all agree that diversity is a good thing and that Manchester is a wealthier community because of it.

(Stewart, 2006)

Multidirectional but not multicultural: incorporation within down-scale neoliberalism

To migrant newcomers to Manchester, multiculturalism has therefore offered mixed messages not only of public celebration, but also of criminalization, disparagement and racialization. Consequently migrants striving to obtain leadership positions and become part of local institutional life have been generally reluctant to engage in public ethnic identity politics. The minimal level of ethnic organizing on the part of migrants in Manchester must be read in relationship to the constrained opportunity structure of a down-scaled city. It is important to note that, while many migrants distanced themselves from the efforts by city leaders to use multiculturalism as part of the implementation of a neoliberal agenda, migrants nonetheless participated in processes of neoliberal restructuring and re-scaling as they established pathways of local and transnational incorporation.

One of the ways that migrants responded to the official and commercial evocations of multiculturalism in Manchester was by publicly organizing global religious institutions and identities, while privately relying on ethnic, familial and work-based networks as well as entrepreneurial activities to develop pathways of local and transnational incorporation. Our study documented that in Manchester, Buddhist, Muslim and Pentecostal Christian migrants created religious institutions that did not publicly highlight the ethnic or national backgrounds of their members.

All the members of the Buddhist Temple in Manchester came from Vietnam and Vietnamese songs and a national flag were part of temple life. Migrants from Vietnam are one of the oldest of the 'new immigrant' populations in Manchester. The first Vietnamese migrants to Manchester came as political refugees immediately after the fall of Saigon in 1975, and the population continued to increase through US refugee programmes and processes of family reunion. However, although city leaders and social service agencies recognized migrants from Vietnam as one of the distinctive 'ethnic groups', temple members went to some lengths to distance themselves from any attempts to consider their temple as the representative of a Vietnamese community.

In addition to the racialization and othering that came with public re-presentations of multiculturalism in Manchester, which were not offset by the provision of resources for community organizing, the temple leadership had other reasons to keep their organization as a private space. Migrants from Vietnam in Manchester were divided by ethnic identity, politics and religion. The temple membership consisted of a network of families that had been considered Chinese in Vietnam, although in Manchester they presented themselves as Vietnamese. This public identity fitted into the broader narrative of US government refugee resettlement that welcomed this population as allies in the war in Vietnam. Migrants from Vietnam acknowledged the multiplicity of their identities within their household and family networks. For example, in the performance of a wedding ceremony, the father of the bride explained to Thad Guldbrandsen that he was wearing a Chinese ritual object because 'this is my house, my wedding'. Visiting extended families Guldbrandsen found that a building with several flats was occupied by an extended family with Chinese-speaking grandparents who provided childcare. He also visited a young couple whose parents both came from Hue but had different ethnic backgrounds. They were teaching their children to speak both Vietnamese and Chinese, as well as English.

In New York City, 'ethnic groups' of populations known as 'communities', such as Haitians, are equally diverse with political, linguistic, cultural and religious divisions (Glick Schiller & Fouron, 2001). However, the city provided a funding and resource structure that supported state-initiated multicultural community organizing and then its neoliberal reconfiguration. In a very different terrain Vietnamese in Manchester chose to highlight their religious differences, not in the form of ethno-religious diversity, but in relationship to their more encompassing global religious identities of Buddhist, Catholic and Protestant.

For example, some of the migrants from Vietnam in Manchester were Catholic and participated in the Vietnamese-language masses in one of the parishes. Masses, especially on occasions such as Christmas and Easter, were occasions for all generations to dress in their finest and meet and greet other Vietnamese. However, Vietnamese-language masses were not used by a Vietnamese leadership as a display of cultural difference or as a platform for claiming a more public role in diversity discourses in the city. While the local Catholic leadership encouraged displays of cultural difference by facilitating celebrations such as that of the Virgin of Guadeloupe, a Mexican saint, and inviting other 'nationalities' to participate in an accompanying 'festival', the Vietnamese members of the parish generally shunned such public displays of multiculturalism.

This parish also recognized an organization called the 'Vietnamese Community', but this group tended to keep a low profile during multicultural celebrations in Manchester, outside their parish holy day masses. Members of this organization were a subset of Catholics from Vietnam who remained vehemently anti-communist and were engaged in opposing the current government of Vietnam. Their primary public action in Manchester was a campaign to convince public schools and local organizations to use the flag of

South Vietnam (1954–75) in multicultural activities rather than the current Vietnamese national flag.

Wanting to maintain their transnational familial and business ties in Vietnam and consequently not wanting to be linked to the subversive politics of this organization, other Vietnamese, including the leadership of the temple, sought to differentiate themselves from this 'Vietnamese Community'. In Manchester, transnational family network building initially contributed to the ability of family members to come to Manchester from Vietnam, obtain employment and promotion, and build the temple into a vibrant local institution. At the same time, through transnational marriages and networks members of the temple were increasingly also becoming incorporated in Vietnam.

However, the temple's organizational ties were not to Vietnam directly but to a Buddhist organization with headquarters in San Francisco and chapels in hundreds of cities around the globe. This Buddhist organization popularized Vietnamese Buddhism, but it had a religious identity rather than a nationalist identity. The Buddhist temple in Manchester was only loosely affiliated with this larger Buddhist network, which provided monks who visited occasionally, but did not routinely lead worship.

This indirect connection to Vietnam reflected not only the complexity of the temple members' ethnic identification but also the range of politics within the population, which could not comfortably be represented through the multi-cultural category of 'the Vietnamese community'. Tuan, one of the leaders of the temple, refused to visit Vietnam because of his anti-communist stance and wished to represent this through displays of American patriotism symbolized by the American flag within the space of the temple and professions of loyalty to the United States. Yet, while of Chinese descent he neither repudiated Vietnam – noting that temple members went 'back to our homeland in Vietnam' to get the robes that people wore in the temple – nor accepted an assimilationist US discourse. Tuan said that in the United States: 'we are all from somewhere else. This country belongs to nobody. This country belongs to everybody' (Guldrandsen, fieldwork log, 14 July 2004).

Manchester had one mosque located in rented space in an office building. Although South Asians predominated, those who prayed at the mosque had diverse backgrounds and included migrants from Morocco, Jordon, Syria, Iraqi, Egypt, Palestine, Bosnia, Bangladesh, Pakistan, Afghanistan, Malaysia and India. As in the case of the leadership of the Buddhist temple, the leaders of the association that organized the mosque also sought a non-ethnicized religious identity as an aspect of their public self-representation in Manchester. Mosque members also resembled temple members in the ways their religious persona complemented the various personal pathways of incorporation that individual members sought within the neoliberal restructuring of the city. The head of the association was a respected economics professor at a local university. His leadership of the mosque gave him some campus-wide status; however, he did not emerge as a public figure within the multicultural activities developed by city leaders.

City and state political leaders and officials in Manchester approached the mosque as both a site of multicultural representation and as a threat that needed to be kept under surveillance and contained. After September 11, the mayor, police chief and New Hampshire attorney general made visits to the mosque. Their speeches all assured members of the mosque that Muslims were welcome in Manchester as part of the multicultural fabric of the city. However, members of the mosque knew that multicultural acceptance came with the positing of foreign difference and estrangement. They knew this because the FBI also visited the mosque and because the mosque was forced to engage in a long legal struggle to obtain land and permission to erect a purpose-built house of prayer.

Consequently, although the mosque leadership did not participate in Manchester multicultural activities or representations, after the growth of public anti-Islamic sentiments in the wake of September 11, 2001, there were occasions when speakers at the mosque signalled their participation in broader US-oriented identity politics and inserted within it a Muslim identity. However, rather than accepting either a cultural affiliation such as South Asian (the majority of the mosque but certainly not its sole ethnicity) or highlight the mosque as part of the religious pluralism of the city – which would have been welcomed in the city's heralding of diversity – the mosque leadership encouraged worshippers to understand the Muslim experience as similar to the experience of being black in America. On one such occasion, a visiting imam spoke to the approximately ninety men and a handful of women who sat on the carpeted floor of the mosque (the women separated by a curtain) by reading a long quotation from Martin Luther King's 1967 speech 'Where do we go from here: Chaos or community?' Before the quotation, the imam asks his listeners to substitute 'Muslim' for 'Negro' and note how well it fits with the current situation. The quotation used powerful metaphors to describe the mechanism of blaming the victim.

> Being a Negro in America means trying to smile when you want to cry. It means trying to hold on to physical life amid psychological death. It means the pain of watching your children grow up with clouds of inferiority in their mental skies. It means having your legs cut off, and then being condemned for being a cripple. It means seeing your mother and father spiritually murdered by the slings and arrows of daily exploitation, and then being hated for being an orphan.

The imam went on to say 'strong words' – but they in many ways reflect the position of Muslims in American society today – and urged the mosque members to organize in order to obtain civil rights. To invoke Martin Luther King in this way highlighted historical US racialized divisions and domains of struggle and posed Muslims as the disenfranchised and disempowered, rather than as part of an inclusive US cultural mosaic.

As in the case of the Buddhist temple leadership, when the mosque leadership did promote a public religious identity, they positioned themselves within a global religion rather than as part of a multicultural America. Transborder ties and identities are of course a significant aspect of historical and contemporary Islam. In the case of this particular mosque, these ties were highlighted not only through the pilgrimages some members made to Mecca, but also through weak but present transnational religious networks. During our research, for example, the prayer leaders for Ramadan included second-generation Pakistanis from London. Local incorporation in Manchester was also framed through the universality of Islam and its mission to transmit the word of Allah. The mosque included converts, who were white New Hampshire women who married North African men and then converted to Islam.

Many migrants became incorporated in the city through fundamentalist Christian churches and an evangelical religious network that emphasized the shared Christian identity of their members, rather than their cultural differences. Christian migrants found that these churches gave them local and transnational networks that connected them to local political leaders, as well as a vibrant local support network that provided employment, resources and social capital. In the course of the study, increasing numbers of Catholic migrants joined these churches because they offered wider incorporative possibilities offered to newcomers, in a city with so little public or charitable social supports. In contrast, during the years of our research the Manchester Catholic leadership offered migrants a form of multiculturalist worship and little substantive support.[4] There were masses in various languages including Spanish, Vietnamese and French, and an 'African mass' – a division not by culture or language but by a difference that simultaneously racialized African difference and recognized their need for succour against the racialization they experienced in the city. There was some effort to organize religious activities that reflected the backgrounds of parishioners such as the festival of the Mexican Virgin of Guadeloupe.

Many of the evangelizing Christian congregations rejected divisions by culture and race, drawing instead a line between those on the side of God and those allied with the devil. This division has allowed migrants to legitimize their presence and social citizenship in the city as believers whose mission is to bring the word of Jesus to the city. A significant actor in this Christian pathway of incorporation was a Nigerian pastor, Heaven's Gift. In a city such as Manchester with only a handful of Nigerians divided among Protestants, Catholics and Muslims, it would have been difficult for Heaven's Gift to organize a separate Nigerian congregation. However, there were several hundred African Protestants in Manchester and the multicultural discourse of Manchester would have been supportive of an African church. Instead, Heaven's Gift formed a network in the greater Manchester area that grew to encompass more than twenty churches, ranging from fundamentalist to Con-gregationalist congregations, all committed to the conservative values of patriarchal families and the rejection of homosexuality and abortion.

The network, the Resurrection Crusade, was dedicated to winning the city of Manchester for God. Most of the member congregations in the network were composed primarily of white natives. However the network included a Spanish-speaking church and an African-American congregation, both of which made their Christian rather than their ethnic or pan-ethnic identity primary. Heaven's Gift himself belonged to a 'home church' that was mostly white working-class but included in its ranks a Ghanaian Harvard graduate and Iraqi and Sudanese refugee families.

The Crusade was more than an organizational nexus. It had its own individual activists, who pulled members of their own personal networks into an expanding field of Christian activity and connection. Between 2002 and 2005, migrants from all over the world increasingly joined the social field that was constructed and expanded by Heaven's Gift and his core activists. The number of migrants in the core also increased. About 20 per cent of those who attended prayer conferences, breakfasts and events sponsored by the Crusade were migrants of African, Caribbean, Latin American and Asian origin. In 2005, the Crusade established a prayer centre in an office building in the central business district of Manchester – the area in which most of the efforts to revive the city's fortunes were concentrated.

When the Crusade leadership spoke of building community, their vision was one of encompassment rather than enclosure. They extended their network into the domains of politics with considerable success because the agenda of the Crusade resonated within broader political projects that had great legitimacy at the beginning of the twenty-first century in Manchester, the United States, and the homelands of many of the migrants. Locally, political and business leaders were receptive to public displays of religious fervour and welcomed opportunities to align themselves with Christian pastors who expressed concern for the moral state of the city and the world. These local political leaders also favoured public representations of ethnic and racial diversity, and the activities of the Crusade provided them with publicity, a morality discourse and an audience that appeared diverse.

At the same time, nationally and internationally, President George W. Bush and his neoconservative allies both in and out of government were preaching the global application of Christian values. In this setting, the Crusade built networks that linked members – migrants and natives alike – to local and state-level Republican and Democratic politicians. The New Hampshire governor in 2004, who was a conservative Republican and strong Bush supporter, personally attended the Manchester Community Prayer Breakfast of the Crusade. Mayor Baines, a Democrat and a Catholic, attended the breakfasts from 2003 to 2005 and developed an ongoing relationship to the Crusade.

When he first came in contact with the Crusade, Baines imagined the network to be primarily immigrant in composition and gave speeches and made proclamations that situated the Crusade within the parameters of Manchester's public multiculturalism. He praised the newcomers who, through their factory work, contributed to the strength of the city's economy. He went on to celebrate Manchester's new 'colorful mosaic', noting that Manchester welcomed 'new immigrants from Central America, South America, Asia, Africa, and Central Europe'. At his first message to a Crusade prayer breakfast Baines stated:

Manchester experienced an infusion of energy and vitality that has contributed to a sense of rebirth, where people from all ethnicities and religious backgrounds come together to form a new and exciting community. We celebrate the diversity of Manchester and embrace the fact that people from all over the world come to our wonderful city to find the freedom to practice the religion of their heritage.

(Baines, n.d.)

This narrative stood in sharp contradiction to the pathway of local and transnational incorporation through born-again Christianity that was being pursued by the migrants who participated in the prayer breakfasts and prayer conferences. By the 2005 prayer breakfasts, Baines had gotten the message. He abandoned his talk of diversity and workers and publicly thanked God and the Crusade's prayer intercession for the miraculous recovery of his ill granddaughter.

The mayor and others who controlled public resources also facilitated the incorporation of the Crusade into the religious and political life of the city. The mayor welcomed Crusade members to City Hall each year for the National Day of Prayer, allowed the Crusade to pray in the aldermanic chambers in 2005, and made it possible for the Crusade to hold yearly prayer programmes in a city park, for which the city provided a band shell, speaker system and police protection. Police and firemen also participated in the event. Through its political networks the Crusade was also given access to a weekly show on local public community television; Heaven's Gift was the featured preacher.

In Manchester fundamentalist churches offered some Christian migrants a pathway of incorporation into the life of the city, the country and the world that few other institutions in those cities were able to provide. These migrants found themselves cast as simultaneously dangerous, as well as useful colourful bodies that represented a necessary but ambivalent component for marketing the city as a global actor. By choosing to emphasize a Christian universalism rather than an ethnic particularism, Christian migrants responded to this positioning by seeking different ways to become incorporated as local and global actors on their own terms, beyond multiculturalist discourse.

Neoliberal local and transnational incorporation

Of course neoliberal strategies of governance also recognized religious community as a form of self-regulating difference through which individuals can be disciplined. From positions of unequal power, the migrant leadership of the mosque, the temple and the Christian network contested the imposition of categories of radical cultural difference in dramatically different ways. The Buddhist temple resisted public acclaim, an ethnic label or strong national and transnational organizational ties to a global religious network. The mosque resolutely maintained an open door policy, welcoming official visitors and researchers while exploring idioms of oppositional positioning that put them within the US political discourse of race and civil rights without the pejorative labelling of radical cultural difference. Given the public acceptance and privileging of Christianity in Manchester, the Christian fundamentalist migrants could most fully embrace a global religious identity and network and use it as a means of entry into the city that did not confine migrant members within multicultural difference.

However, in similar ways the migrant members of all of these religious organizations built outward from their religious organization to seize the limited but still significant opportunities afforded them by neoliberal restructuring of the city. Without the possibility of obtaining resources for settlement and to sustain a leadership structure through ethnic organization, they nonetheless found pathways of local and transnational incorporation within neoliberal economic policies and its accompanying values of individual consumerism. In so doing, migrants in Manchester emerged as both agents of locally instituted neoliberalism and its reconstitution and contestation.

As indicated above, Manchester urban developers initially saw the availability of cheap docile labour as one of the assets of the city's neoliberal production regime that developed after 1991 as part of the ongoing post-Fordist structuring of the global economy. The industries in Manchester, built through a migrant workforce, developed or grew because of their ability to supply relatively cheap, non-unionized, malleable labour in small patriarchal non-union plants. Interviews with migrants associated with the temple, the Christian network, the mosque and the Catholic church indicated the contradictory ways in which some migrants used an exploitive, minimally regulated factory system as a means of economic or social mobility. We found important interconnections between the ways in which networks based in the Buddhist temple and the Christian Crusade connected migrant workers to factory supervisors or individuals with higher positions in the factory.

While these factories maintained high levels of exploitation, unsafe conditions and long hours, they also offered a personalized style of labour-management relationships. By developing individual relationships to management, migrants in these workplaces found opportunities that facilitated their local and transnational incorporation. For example, a shop foreman in the organizing core of the Crusade helped place believers in factory jobs or more desirable shifts. Through these personal faith-based ties migrants not only obtained employment but also were able to some extent to mitigate their working conditions. The fact that at some workplaces there was no coterie of co-ethnics to assist a newly arriving migrant, especially when new migrating populations began to arrive in Manchester, facilitated the formation of this alternative type of social capital, providing workers with connections to people with more access to resources, knowledge about the city and society and influential social connections.

This pattern made all the difference for several of the first Vietnamese who settled in Manchester. For example, Tuan, a member of the Nguyen family, was able to approach John, an engineer who was a white native of New Hampshire, and ask him to sponsor Tuan's family. John agreed to co-sponsor Tuan's parents, several of his siblings and their nuclear families. When they arrived John became incorporated into the Nguyen extended family network and he is visibly noticeable in photographs of engagement parties and birthday parties. In a way, John became the family genealogist, creating a spreadsheet of family members and sending birthday cards to family members.

Migrants also participated, were influenced by and contributed to other efforts by the city officials and promoters to implement the neoliberal agenda in order to redevelop and re-scale the city. These efforts included the redevelopment of the city centre and the facilitation of home ownership through sub-prime mortgages. Elsewhere I have described the way migrant entrepreneurs can play a significant role in providing the small businesses needed to revitalize the city centre (Glick Schiller & Çağlar, 2011). In Manchester, migrant businesses formed a disproportionately high number of the small shops on the high street. Migrants also became an important component of the sub-prime mortgage market and their ability to obtain low-income mortgages facilitated the gentrification of decaying high-crime neighbourhoods. A local public agency worked to encourage and facilitate home ownership in Manchester among migrants. Their website and publicity made it clear that they included non-whites (that is to say, in Manchester, new immigrants) among their clients. Real estate agents found willing customers among members of many migrant populations in Manchester, who used their extended family networks to facilitate buying apartments and homes, thereby contributing to and participating in the rising property market of the 1990s to 2005.

Heaven's Gift's Christian networks facilitated his ability to obtain a sub-prime mortgage as part of the general funding of migrants as agents to stabilize and gentrify neighbourhoods in the city. The Buddhist and factory-based networks that enabled extended Vietnamese family networks to settle led to family regrouping that facilitated home ownership. The title of multi-flat buildings in which members of extended Vietnamese families lived were often held by one family member, whose parents, siblings and other relatives paid a modest rent to defray the costs of the mortgage. To the outside observer, this house or cluster of houses might look like an ethnic enclave; in point of fact they housed members of an extended family. Muslim Bosnian migrants did not pool capital for home ownership through extensive family networks but did pool kin-based resources to buy two-family houses. Advice on property acquisition and management was obtained through various networks that ranged from mosque-based ties to Manchester locals met as co-workers in factories. The ability to purchase housing without having to accumulate a considerable down payment allowed family members not only to house themselves, but also to accumulate capital through the pooling of family resources in the gentrifying Manchester housing market.

This capital accumulation facilitated migrants' ability to also become incorporated transnationally, purchasing land, houses and business in rising property markets that were being transformed through neoliberal agendas in their home countries. For example, one Vietnamese family in Manchester invested substantial resources in building, or helping to build, at least three houses in Vietnam. Thuy and Chung, who both were working on factory lines, paid Chung's brother in Vietnam $4000 to buy a house, $4000 to the brother of his deceased sister to build a house and several thousand dollars for a house and store for Thuy's mother. All of this is in addition to the regular remittances they sent for daily family needs and education costs of children and college students. If we take the extended family, rather than individuals or 'the community' as the unit of analysis, we can see that these family networks created a transnational social field that gave their members a certain material stake in the neoliberal economies in two states. They were dually and simultaneously incorporated through their investment in housing.

At the same time, while migrants became eager converts to the neoliberal vision of social mobility through home ownership, their opposing of global religious affiliations to public multiculturalism contained aspects of contestation. The value system of these religions provided them with a potential base to question individualism and unbridled consumption and vast economic disparity. These tensions developed further as the weaknesses of the global and local neoliberal project became clear. Beginning in 2005, property prices began to fall and migrants found that they could no longer readily sell houses and get a price higher or even equivalent to what they had paid. Foreclosures began, and then increased, over the next few years. There were increasing factory closures or lay-offs, although the pattern was uneven and one of the most exploitive factories in the area reopened in 2008 and used its ties with migrant networks to recruit labour. The employment situation was grim enough that a Congolese migrant who had lost two finger tips in a machine on which the safety guard had been removed encouraged his daughter to work in the plant. It became almost impossible for migrants who had trained as home health-care attendants to find work as the competition for low-wage low-status jobs became even more intense. There were also reports of migrants leaving the area in pursuit of better employment possibilities.

In 2009 the city website still promoted its most recent slogan 'birthplace of your American dream'. While business planning for the city still projected economic development as a possibility of the city, the dream that Manchester was promoting seemed not to be multicultural. In a comprehensive business plan for the city published in that year, the immigrants and refugees were mentioned only four times and always in relationship to poverty rather than culture. Readers were informed that:

> though it has many strengths, it should also be noted that Manchester has the
> state's largest concentration of individuals and families in poverty, a large refugee
> and immigrant population, an older housing stock and many neighborhoods in

need of improvement. Given these factors, it is important that the City develop a focused economic development strategy that comprehensively addresses its unique opportunities, challenges and needs.

(Manchester Office of Economic Development, 2009)

The terms 'cultural diversity' or 'multiculturalism' were nowhere to be seen. However, the migrants from all over the world were still in Manchester and more refugees were arriving.

Conclusion

Many scholars have argued that neoliberalism, while it might have taken the form of an ideology with global reach, has been implemented in diverse ways depending on the historical trajectories of different regions, states and localities (Brenner & Theodore, 2002; England & Ward, 2007; Ong, 2006). Those writing on multiculturalism have tended to concentrate on national variations in ideology and practice, rather than theorizing variations in trajectories of local implementation (Modood & Werbner, 1997). There have been even fewer attempts to identify the relationship between multicultural policies and practices in a city, the relationship between that city and the efforts of city leadership to become global competitors by instituting neoliberal projects, and the role of migrants within the intersection of multiculturalism and neoliberalism.

In this article I have suggested that exploring migrants' response to, and active role within, the local efforts to implement multicultural discourses as part of the restructuring and re-branding of a city can illuminate aspects of both multiculturalism and neoliberalism. The article calls for an approach to cities as differently positioned regionally, nationally and globally, in terms of the degree to which they were able to reposition themselves as engines of capital generation. That is to say, when discussing neoliberalism and multiculturalism more needs to be said about cities that are not clearly 'world cities' or 'global cities' but have been significantly affected by global flows of capital and people. All cities have been affected by capital restructuring and are in that sense 'global' but not all have been affected in the same way. Moreover, it is not sufficient to speak about cities as 'globalizing' or 'ordinary'; cities that have had little success in restructuring efforts, such as Manchester, New Hampshire, and remain or become down-scaled within processes of local and regional competition offer different possibilities and limitations for migrant settlement, incorporation and transnational connection than do cities with greater degrees of economic, cultural and political capital (Amin & Graham, 1997; Marcuse & van Kempen, 2000; Robinson, 2006).

In the case of Manchester, New Hampshire, I have demonstrated that multicultural discourses have been part of the effort of the city leadership to restructure and re-scale their city. The city leaders saw the new arrivals as an embodiment of multiculturalism. They perceived physical difference and

RIGHTS, CULTURES, SUBJECTS AND CITIZENS

equated it with discrete cultural identities. This discourse had local effects, including processes of ethnogenesis. In Manchester refugees from the former Yugoslavia began learning to be Bosnians, an identity that did not fully exist when they fled the death and destruction in their homeland. People from Vietnam, who had been marked socially and politically as of Chinese descent, began to signal that they were Vietnamese. However, without the possibility that culturally marked identities could provide access to social services, social mobility or political positions, migrants tended not to use such identities as their primary means of incorporation into the city.

While migrants could obtain some recognition from city political leaders and officials as public foreigners who embodied cultural difference, this very prominent embodiment was simultaneously a form of racialization and hier-archical differentiation. There were a few individuals who chose this path and sought to organize their 'ethnic group'. Generally, while the listing of these groups became part of the public fostering of multiculturalism by social service agencies, most ethnic community organizations had little long-term viability. The exceptions were organizations involved almost exclusively in long-distance nationalist projects such as the 'Vietnamese' community and these organiza-tions were mistrusted by most of the migrants the leaders claimed to represent.

Instead, in Manchester migrants used organizations linked to global religions as a means of social and emotional support, and as intermediaries between their migrant backgrounds and the need to build local networks of incorporation. The migrants in the Buddhist Temple, the Islamic Association and the Resurrection Crusade all promoted values that were surprisingly resonant with the values of natives of New Hampshire whom migrants came to know as co-workers and through intermarriage. This publicly delineated value system included the 'sanctity of the family', 'intact families', 'respect for elders and women', 'the power of prayer', as well as paternal authority, heterosexu-ality and chastity. Increasingly, after the year 2000 public discourse promoted by public officials, public schools and local organizations in the city also emphasized neoconservative values. However, Protestant Christian organiza-tions and identities proved to be the most successful vector of migrant in-corporation, since they not only placed migrants in the mainstream Christian culture both locally and nationally but situated them as the voice of main-stream values.

At the very same time, as long as neoliberal economics remained apparently vibrant, the growing public discourse of a Christian neoconservatism did not undercut, but was synergistic with, many aspects of the local implementation of a neoliberal agenda, including its promotion of the city as culturally diverse. Migrants responded to efforts to develop the city centre and to increase local property values by creating a class of migrant home owners that worked as a force for stabilizing and gentrifying urban neighbourhoods. Soon incorporated into regimes of capital accumulation through private property, migrants used the growth of the sub-prime mortgage industry as a means of supporting family, both locally and transnationally, and further accumulating local and transnational capital.

Migrants were disciplined by the labour practices of patriarchally adminis-
tered small factories, but also used this labour regime to build their networks
of incorporation and sustain their kin. This form of labour management
restrained workers' protest against unsafe and illegal working conditions and
terms of employment because networks in the factory linked professionals in
the factory and foremen with significant members of kin networks. At the same
time these networks facilitated the hiring of a migrant's kin since hiring as well
as labour management was done through personal ties.

It is unclear what the economic downturn and crisis of neoliberal forms
of capital accumulation will mean in terms of the local configuration of multiculturalism, neoliberalism and neoconservatism in Manchester. Aspects of the
religious value system that condemn hedonism and endorse community support
may become more prominent and lead to more vocal calls for social justice and
redistribution of wealth. It was apparent in public declarations and private
conversations that a yearning for social equality was central to members' values
and motivated some of their religious practices. It is also unclear how the faltering
of both neoliberalism and multiculturalism will affect the trajectories of migrant
incorporation in a city that was already struggling before the crisis began.

Notes

1   This research was conducted with support from the McArthur Foundation Human
Security Programme, a Saul O. Sidore award and a James H. Hayes and Claire Short
Hayes professorship from the Center for Humanities of the University of New
Hampshire. My thanks go to Bert Feintuch and Peter Wade for their support and
encouragement and Thad Guldbrandsen for his work as a co-researcher. Thanks also to
the many migrants and refugees who contributed to this paper and because of
commitment of confidentiality are represented only by pseudonyms. A draft of this
paper was delivered at a conference of the Centre for Research on Socio-Cultural
Change (CRESC) of the University of Manchester.
2   I use the word 'migrant' to include both immigrants and refugees, despite the
fact that they have different entitlements and refugees in the United States have a faster
and less costly track to citizenship. In Manchester, many people who arrived with
permanent resident or student visas came from war-torn countries. People with various
entry statuses are often members of the same networks, organizations or families, share
workplaces and place of worship and are served by many of the same organizations.
3   One 'minority' organization, which was initiated by professionals including some of
immigrant background, did succeed in obtaining various kinds of public funding to
provide health education and linkages to services. Persons from various immigrant
and refugee backgrounds were hired to do 'community outreach'. Income was earned
through providing cultural competency classes for officials and businesses.
4   An elderly French-Canadian nun tried to provide much needed food, clothing and
furniture for newly arrived refugees. Masses also have been developed in Portuguese
and Polish. More recently an internal evaluation by the Archdiocese recognized this
problem and 'in the face of financial setbacks, the diocese put multicultural issues in the
forefront when making decisions about how to restructure diocesan services and parish
mergers and closings' (Diocese of Manchester, n.d., p. 1).

References

Amin, A. & Graham, S. (1997). The ordinary city. *Transactions of the Institute of British Geographers, 22*(4), 411–29.

Baber, H. E. (2008). *The multicultural mystique: The liberal case against diversity.* Amherst, NY: Prometheus Books.

Baines, R. (n.d.). Letter to prayer conference. In possession of Nina Glick Schiller, Department of Social Anthropology, University of Manchester, UK.

Basch, L., Glick Schiller, N. & Szanton Blanc, C. (1994). *Nations unbound: Transnational projects, post-colonial predicaments and deterritorialized nation-states.* Amsterdam: Gordon & Breach.

Benmayor, R., Torruellas, R. & Juarbe, A. (1992). Responses to poverty among Puerto Rican women: Identity, community, and cultural citizenship. Joint Committee for Public Policy Research on Contemporary Hispanic Issues of the Inter-University Program for Latino Research and the Social Science Research Council. Centro de Estudios Puertorriqueños, Hunter College, City University of New York.

Brandtstädter, S., Wade, P. & Woodward, K. (2008). Special issue outline. Unpublished.

Brenner, N. & Theodore, N. (2002). Cities and the geographies of actually existing neoliberalism. In N. Brenner & N. Theodore (Eds.), *Spaces of neoliberalism: Urban restructuring in North America and Western Europe* (pp. 2–32). Oxford: Blackwell.

Brubaker, R. (2001). The return of assimilation? Changing perspectives on immigration and its sequels in France, Germany and the United States. *Ethnic and Racial Studies, 24*(4), 531–48.

Castles, S. & Davidson, A. (2000). *Citizenship and migration.* London: Routledge.

Davis, D. (2005). Davis calls for rethink on multiculturalism. Retrieved 22 March 2009 from http://www.guardian.co.uk/politics/2005/aug/03/conservatives.britishidentit

Diocese of Manchester. (n.d.). *Best practices report – Diocese of Manchester.* Retrieved 8 May 2009 from http://www.usccb.org/mrs/ManchesterBestPracticesReport.pdf

Eastman, H. (1896). *Semi-centennial of the City of Manchester, New Hampshire September 6, 7, 8, 9, 1896.* Compiled under direction of Hon. William C. Clarke, Mayor, Hon. Edgar J. Knowlton, [and] Edward J. Burnham, Manchester, NH: Committee on Publication.

England, K. & Ward, K. (Eds.) (2007). *Neoliberalization: States, networks, people.* Oxford: Blackwell.

Florida, R. (2002). *The rise of the creative class: And how it's transforming work, leisure, community and everyday life.* New York: Basic Books.

Gittell, R. (2001). *Manufacturing: New Hampshire's secret strength building on our advantage.* NH SBDC Manufacturing Management Center. Retrieved 22 December 2005 from www.nhsbdc.org/2001%20Manuf%20Report.pdf.

Glick Schiller, N. (2005). Transnational social fields and imperialism: Bringing a theory of power to transnational studies. *Anthropological Theory and Society, 5*(4), 439–61.

Glick Schiller, N. & Çağlar, A. (2009). Towards a comparative theory of locality in migration studies: Migrant incorporation and the city scale. *Journal of Ethnic and Migration Studies, 35*(2), 177–202.

Glick Schiller, N. & Çağlar, A. (2011). Down-scaled cities and migrant pathways: Locality and agency without an ethnic lens. In N. Glick Schiller & A. Çağlar, *Locating migration: Rescaling cities and migrants.* Ithaca, NY: Cornell University Press.

Glick Schiller, N. & Fouron, G. (2001). *Georges woke up laughing: Long distance nationalism and the search for home.* Durham, NC: Duke University Press.

Glick Schiller, N., DeWind, J., Brutus, M. L., Charles, C., Fouron, G. & Thomas, L. (1987). All in the same boat? Unity and diversity among Haitian immigrants. In C. Sutton & E. M. Chaney (Eds.), *Caribbean life in New York City* (pp. 167–84). Staten Island, NY: Center for Migration Studies.

Glick Schiller, N., Çağlar, A. & Guldbrandsen, T. C. (2006). Beyond the ethnic lens: Locality, globality, and born-again incorporation. *American Ethnologist, 33*(4), 612–33.

Greater Manchester Chamber of Commerce. (2009). About Manchester and NH. Retrieved 8 February 2009 from http://www.manchesterareacolleges.com/manchester-area/about-manchester-and-nh.asp

Hall, S. (1980 [1973]). Encoding/decoding. In Centre for Contemporary Cultural Studies (Ed.), *Culture, media, language: Working papers in cultural studies, 1972–79* (pp. 128–38). London: Hutchinson.

Hall, S. (1987). The toad in the garden: Thatcherism amongst the theorists. In C. Nelson & L. Grossberg (Eds.), *Marxism and the interpretation of culture.* London: Macmillan.

Hareven, T. K. & Langenbach, R. (1995). *Amoskeag: Life and work in an American factory-city.* Lebanon, NH: University Press of New England.

Harvey, D. (2005). *Brief history of neoliberalism.* New York: Oxford University Press.

Harvey, D. (2006). *Spaces of global capitalism: Towards a theory of uneven geographical development.* London: Verso.

Huntington, S. (1996). *The clash of civilizations and the remaking of world order.* New York: Touchstone.

Jessop, B. (2002). The political economy of scale. In M. Perkmann & N.-L. Sum (Eds.), *Globalization, regionalization, and cross-border regions* (pp. 25–49). Basingstoke: Macmillan Palgrave.

Manchester Office of Economic Development. (2009). City of Manchester, NH, February 2009. Retrieved 27 March 2009 from http://

www.yourmanchesternh.com/uploads/documents/Manchester%20NH%20CEDS%20Final.pdf.

Marcuse, P. & van Kempen, R. (2000). *Globalizing cities: A new spatial order?* London: Wiley-Blackwell.

Modood, T. (2007). *Multiculturalism: A civic idea.* Oxford: Polity Press.

Modood, T. & Werbner, P. (Eds.) (1997). *The politics of multiculturalism in the new Europe: Racism, identity and community.* London: Zed Books.

Ong, A. (2006). *Neoliberalism as exception: Mutations in citizenship and sovereignty.* Durham, NC: Duke University Press.

Parekh, B. (2000). The report of the Commission on the Future of Multi-Ethnic Britain. Retrieved 20 March 2009 from http://www.runnymedetrust.org/projects/past-projects/meb/report.html

Peck, J. (1998). Geographies of governance: TECs and the neoliberalisation of 'local interests'. *Space and Polity, 2*(1), 5–31.

Robinson, J. (2006). *Ordinary cities: Between modernity and development.* New York: Routledge.

Rosaldo, R. (1989). *Culture and truth: The remaking of social analysis.* Boston, MA: Beacon.

Sennett, R. (1998). *The corrosion of character: The personal consequences of work in the new capitalism.* New York: Norton.

Stewart, W. (2006). Multicultural Manchester: The changing faces of the queen city. *HippoPress,* 28 September.

Takaki, R. (1993). *A different mirror: A history of multicultural America.* New York: Little, Brown.

US Department of Labor. (2005). Bureau of Labor Statistics data. Retrieved from http://data.bls.gov/PDQ/servlet/SurveyOutputServlet?series_id=LNS14000000.

Williams, R. (1958). *Culture and society, 1780–1950.* New York: Columbia University Press.

'Emancipation' or 'regulation'? Law, globalization and indigenous peoples' rights in post-war Guatemala

Rachel Sieder

Abstract

During the last two decades processes of legal globalization have led to the increasing codification of the collective rights of indigenous peoples. In Latin America this shift towards 'codifying culture' began with a series of constitutional reforms during the 1990s which recognized a series of rights of indigenous people and the ratification by many states of the International Labour Organization's Convention 169 on the rights of indigenous and tribal peoples. For many, this regional 'neoliberal multicultural' turn (Hale, 2002, 2006) was not about recognizing rights as such, but rather heralded a series of governmental policies signalling limited acceptance of cultural diversity which ultimately facilitated transnational forms of capitalist accumulation.

The limited gains of state-endorsed multiculturalism and the threats posed to indigenous livelihoods by the current commodities boom have encouraged a growing number of counter-hegemonic legal engagements, or legal globalization 'from below', which resort to ever more transnationalized legal pluralities (Santos & Rodríguez-Garavito, 2005). Indigenous people across Latin America continue to judicialize their protests, appealing to legal entitlements, including both 'hard law' (treaty and constitutional law) and 'soft law' (such as the internal norms of multilateral development institutions), in order to claim greater autonomy and protest against the effects of dominant patterns of economic development. Using Boaventura de Sousa Santos's heuristic device of the regulatory and emancipatory dimensions of law (Santos, 1998, 2002), in this article I examine the effects of legal globalization and the appropriation of legal instruments and discourses by indigenous people in post-war Guatemala. Specifically, I highlight the distinct legal frameworks, and conflicting notions of property, development, citizenship and democratic participation and voice at play in recent mobilizations against mining projects. The conclusions reflect on the possible effects of judicializing indigenous peoples' political demands.

Keywords: legal globalization; indigenous peoples; rights; law; Guatemala; multiculturalism.

During the last two decades processes of legal globalization have led to the increasing codification of the collective rights of indigenous peoples. In Latin America this shift towards 'codifying culture' took the form of constitutional reforms implemented during the 1990s which recognized a series of rights of indigenous people and the ratification by many states of International Labour Organization's Convention 169 on the rights of indigenous and tribal peoples. For many, this regional 'neoliberal multicultural' turn (Hale, 2002, 2006) was not about recognizing rights as such, but rather heralded a series of governmental policies signalling limited acceptance of cultural diversity which ultimately facilitated transnational forms of capitalist accumulation.

The limited gains of state-endorsed multiculturalism and the threats posed to indigenous livelihoods by the current commodities boom have encouraged a growing number of counter-hegemonic legal engagements, or legal globalization 'from below', which resort to ever more transnationalized legal pluralities (Santos & Rodríguez-Garavito, 2005). Indigenous people in Latin America continue to judicialize their protests, appealing to legal entitlements, including both 'hard law' (treaty and constitutional law) and 'soft law' (such as the internal norms of multilateral development institutions), in order to claim greater autonomy and protest against the effects of dominant patterns of economic development. Using Boaventura de Sousa Santos's heuristic device of the regulatory and emancipatory dimensions of law (Santos 1998, 2002), in this article I examine the effects of such legal globalization and the appropriation of legal instruments and discourses by indigenous people in post-war Guatemala. Specifically, I highlight the distinct legal frameworks and conflicting notions of property, development, citizenship and democratic participation and voice at play in recent mobilizations against mining projects. In the final section I reflect on the possible effects of judicializing indigenous peoples' political demands.

The 'emancipatory' and 'regulatory' dimensions of law

Boaventura de Sousa Santos adopts a useful heuristic device – the idea of emancipation versus regulation – to signal the paradoxes of legal instruments (1998, 2002). Law clearly encompasses regulatory and repressive elements as well as emancipatory potentials. By codifying rights and setting out the obligations of states to uphold those rights, law raises the prospect that those rights will be enforced. In this sense it holds out a utopian promise and has long been invoked by the weak and marginalized – for example, appeals to the ideal of citizenship by those, such as women or slaves, who were systematically denied formal citizenship rights. Today international human rights law holds out that utopian and emancipatory promise to peoples across the world. Although we can date the emergence of global human rights to the middle of the twentieth century, the last two decades have witnessed the global spread of international human right norms and 'rights consciousness' – 'a willingness, or eagerness, to make use of institutions (like courts) which enforce rights, or which decide when rights have been infringed on or broken' (Friedman, 2002, p. 38) and to deploy legal discourses and mechanisms as part of political and social struggles.[1] This has occurred in tandem with a related global trend for national constitutions to enumerate ever greater numbers of rights (Tate & Vallinder, 1995). Transitions from authoritarian to democratic regimes have frequently involved the drafting of new constitutions and these increasingly incorporate not only political and civil, but also social, economic and cultural rights, often with hundreds of articles setting out the precise obligations incumbent on states to uphold and defend them. This codification of ever greater numbers of rights is also related to the treaty commitments of the states in question. Governments' endorsement of internationally sanctioned human rights instruments signals their desire to sign up for membership of the international community; it does not of course prove their willingness or indeed their ability to guarantee those rights in practice.

Such developments have both encouraged and been driven by a marked tendency for social movements to frame specific political struggles in terms of more general legal entitlements. Rights consciousness is a key factor in explaining the growth of strategic litigation or the deployment of rights discourses by different social actors. The acquisition of 'legal literacy' is often intentionally promoted across national boundaries, for example through support by northern foundations and NGOs to southern-based human rights organizations. (A signal example is the work of the Ford Foundation in supporting human rights NGOs engaged in pioneering social action litigation.)[2] The combination of new legal opportunity structures and growing rights consciousness means that processes of grassroots-driven judicialization – or judicialization 'from below' – are in evidence in a range of different contexts.[3] Social movements, often organized in so-called transnational action networks or TANs, have engaged in counter-hegemonic legal actions, appealing to inter-national norms and the principles of law in order to stake their material, political or cultural claims and fight against oppression, violence and impunity within their nation-states and communities. Such dynamics have been theorized as part of 'boomerang' or 'spiral' models, whereby social movements engage internationally or transnationally in order to bring pressure to bear on their governments and effect change (Keck & Sikkink, 1998; Risse et al., 1999). Kathryn Sikkink in particular has analysed the ways in which movements take advantage of and also create legal opportunity structures, which depend on shifting interactions between domestic and international legal frameworks (Sikkink, 2005). Law then, can evidently be a terrain for counter-hegemonic actions or, in Santos' terms, emancipation.

At the same time, we know from critical socio-legal theory and legal anthropology that law is also an instrument of domination and a pervasive means of reproducing patterns of domination and hegemony. Law codifies power relations, defines certain types of personhood and fixes particular identities. Through the process of what Clifford Geertz referred to as 'skeletonization of fact' (1993, p. 170), law reduces complex social processes to a particular set of ontological categories and representations. As Geertz argued, law is 'a distinctive manner of imagining the real' (1993, p. 173) and thus determines which events and interpretations are taken up as legal facts. Legal orders map out specific formulations of interest and understandings of disputes, as well as establishing the regulatory patterns for their settlement. Dominant modes of thought are thus symbolically represented in law, through which central concepts such as property, forms of political participation or rights-bearing persons and entities (legal subjects) are projected. Such constructions also systematically exclude those who do not conform to these ideals or categories.

Yet, while such categories are essential to the perpetuation and legitimacy of the law, in practice legal rules and concepts are open to interpretation. Even as they are 'fixed', at least partially, in specific legal instruments, interpretations and meanings are subject to ongoing contestation and reinterpretation by different actors. This is particularly the case where international norms and rights discourses are used or invoked in order to challenge national laws and situated practices. Legal anthropology has increasingly focused on globalization and transnational processes and there is particular concern with the ways in which universalist ideas and norms, for example about human rights or gender rights, are taken up and articulated in specific contexts (Merry, 2001, 2004, 2006; Goodale & Merry, 2007; Starr & Goodale, 2003; Stephen, 2005; Wilson, 1997, 2000). Legal systems and engagements with the law can therefore be understood as contested sites of meaning where dominant ideals and values provide the framework for contestation and for advancing alternative understandings and practices. In this way law is constantly negotiated and reshaped in a dynamic dialectic between hegemonic projections and counter-hegemonic actions (Santos 1998, 2002; Santos & Rodriguez-Garavito, 2005). Such processes of legal engagement and contestation are far from new. However, today two factors make them increasingly pervasive and complicated. First, the increasingly complex legal pluralism generated by economic and legal globalization and, second, the accelerated fragmentation and de-centring of state sovereignty which has occurred as a consequence of economic globalization and neoliberal policies encouraging ever greater outsourcing of the traditional functions of government.

Globalization has increasingly meant that multiple and overlapping legal spheres or forms of legal ordering extend across and beyond national borders.

It makes less and less sense (if indeed it ever did) for the legal systems of individual nation states to be examined as bounded national entities, as they are inevitably and increasingly affected and shaped by external and transnational phenomenon. As William Twining has noted, 'one consequence of globalization is a tendency to loosen the association of the ideas of law, state, and nation and so to make more salient the multiplicity of legal orderings' (2000, p. 138). These multiple forms of legal ordering include what we would normally identify as 'law'; that is, national state law and public international law. However, they are not confined to these phenomena alone. They also include regulatory regimes, or what some have termed 'transnational legal fields', attaching to processes of free trade–driven economic integration such as the World Trade Organization (WTO) or the North American Free Trade Agreement (NAFTA).[4] Such free trade agreements have implied profound changes to national legal systems and state sovereignty. For example, private companies can now sue national governments in international arbitration if their expected profits are negatively affected by changes in regulatory policies (for example, such as increases in taxes). This effectively allows transnational companies to sidestep national courts and take their claims directly to the much less transparent arena of international arbitration.[5] Indeed, one form of international or transnational legal ordering which has been of particular interest to socio-legal scholars is that of *lex mercatoria*, the supranational, market-oriented contract law used for transnational business – most recently characterized by the spread of international commercial arbitration (Dezaley & Garth, 1996; Teubner, 1997; Trubek *et al.*, 1994).[6] Other examples of new, transnational legal phenomena or 'soft law' linked to economic globalization might include such things as the World Bank Inspection Panel or the WTO arbitration process (Randeria, 2003).[7]

The growth of human rights law has also been closely associated with the current phase of globalization. International human rights norms now form an increasingly dense web of obligations binding states, at least in theory, as an ever greater range of rights are becoming codified as international law. New human rights treaties (for example, on the rights of women, children or indigenous people) and the international forums through which they are monitored, particularly at the United Nations, have become key sites of legal transnationalism (Merry 2004, 2006; Morgan, 2004a, 2004b, 2007; Santamaría, 2008). As I aim to show in this article, indigenous social movements are increasingly using different kinds of law, including unofficial local law, national law, transnational legal orderings and processes, 'soft law' and international law, to challenge dominant patterns of development and government failures to deliver on the promises of multicultural democracy.

The second aspect that complicates critical engagement with the law is the unevenness and fragmentation of state sovereignty. During the nineteenth and much of the twentieth century, the reach of central government in many Latin American counties relied on informal compacts with private actors rather than formal norms enforced by strong state institutions across national territories

(O'Donnell, 1993; Salvatore *et al.*, 2001). From a more functionalist perspective many contemporary commentators signal 'weak states' or 'insufficient rule of law' as policy problems to be addressed in Latin America. Numerous authors have pointed to the acutely uneven reach of law as a defining feature of states in the region. For example, in a much-cited article, Guillermo O'Donnell likened the rule of law in Latin America to a heat map – blue where the rule of law functioned and applied to all citizens, implying an effective state presence and a monopoly over the use of force; green where the state is present but less effective, coexisting with informal, often illegal practices used to exercise governance; and brown where the state is hardly present, the rule of law does not apply and social and political life is dominated by alternative non-state, often highly violent, mechanisms. In most countries in the region the green and brown areas far outweigh the blue (O'Donnell, 1993).[8]

Such uneven reach of the law is undoubtedly a long-term historical phenomenon that responds to deep-rooted structural and social inequalities. However, the neoliberal state in Latin America is characterized by new forms of legal pluralism which are qualitatively different from those of the past. These involve the multiple and overlapping sovereignties linked to economic globalization – state and social, sub-national, national and supranational. They are also characterized by increasingly complex and fragmented patterns of legality and illegality involving both state and non-state actors (Comaroff & Comaroff, 2006).[9] Neoliberal states do not necessarily seek to exercise coercion or jurisdiction evenly across their territory, according to the classic Weberian formulation of monopoly over the legitimate use of force and control of sovereign power in a given territory. Instead, a profound reshaping of relations between state, market and citizen has led to the devolution or ceding of sovereignty to a range of different actors. Neoliberal reforms of the state have increasingly fragmented law and shifted the terrain on which it is (re)produced and contested. These include the decentralization of certain state functions and the emphasis on the 'participation' of civil society actors, aimed at ensuring that they assume responsibility for the production and distribution of social goods. Such processes, which are an essential feature of the neoliberal model of social policy, have led to a blurring in practice between state sovereignty and what Dennis Rodgers (2006) has termed 'social sovereignty'. It is sometimes hard to discern the dividing line between state and non-state actors. This is increasingly the case in the legal field, as responsibility for low-level conflict resolution is devolved to non-state actors through the promotion of non-judicial alternative dispute resolution or – as discussed below – to indigenous peoples who have, at least in theory, been given the right to jurisdictional autonomy via constitutional reforms or the ratification of certain human rights instruments by Latin American states.

The combined effects of globalization and neoliberal reforms have been to de-link law and the state to an unprecedented extent. While this is in part related to the concentration of global power and capital across national borders, it also potentially provides space for social movements to generate new forms of law and political practices. Undoubtedly engagements with dominant legal frameworks can lead to the cooption and demobilization of political demands, and to the sanctioning of certain identities, practices and discourses. Jessica Witchell and I have written previously about the ways in which certain notions of indigenous identity are fixed by international legal instruments and the problematic consequences this entails:

> Indigenous identities ... are effectively being narrated or codified through dominant legal discourses, specifically those of international human rights law and multiculturalism. This has resulted in the projection of an essentialised, idealised and atemporal indigenous identity, the movement's leaders often perceiving such essentialising as tactically necessary in order to secure collective rights for indigenous people.
>
> (Sieder & Witchell, 2001, p. 201)

Yet at the same time, by interacting with international norms (be these 'hard law' or 'soft law'), social movements engage in what Santos and Rodríguez-Garavito have called 'counter-hegemonic globalization', constructing, they maintain, a wider, plural 'subaltern cosmopolitan legality' (2005, pp. 3, 12–18).[10] This may seem a case of David against the juggernaut of hegemonic globalization. Yet through these kinds of engagements indigenous peoples' social movements formulate alternative understandings of citizenship rights, challenging dominant interests in the state or the private sector The effects of these processes are unpredictable and often, cumulatively, impact upon the construction of new dominant legal norms. The seminal work of Balakrishnan Rajagopal in particular has analysed the ways in which social movements in the South interact with international law. As he states, 'social movements seek to construct alternative visions of modernity and development that constitute valid Third World approaches to international law' (Rajagopal, 2003, p. 3). While emphasizing the ways in which international law validates certain types of resistance (such as anti-colonial struggles) while disqualifying others, Rajagopal also observes how 'international law and institutions provide important arenas for social movement action, as they expand the political space available for transformative politics' (2003, p. 23). Other critical socio-legal scholars have similarly focused on the interaction between international norms and social movements. For example, Santos and Rodríguez-Garavito argue that 'subaltern actors are a critical part of processes whereby global rules are defined, as the current contestation over the regulation of water provision and property rights on traditional knowledge bear witness' (2005, p. 11). In the Guatemalan case examined below, I analyse the interplay between indigenous social movements and national and international norms concerning exploitation of subsoil resources, considering the balance between the 'emancipation' and 'regulation' involved in such subaltern legal engagements.

Codifying 'culture': indigenous rights and the law in Latin America

The codification of rights in law is singularly important because it shapes the *formal* parameters and spaces for popular mobilization and struggle. Throughout the 1980s and 1990s, Latin American constitutionalism experienced a quantum shift as the region's indigenous peoples were recognized through a series of reforms to existing charters or new constitutions. While the specific content of these reforms varied from country to country, they all recognized society as 'multicultural', extending a series of recognitions and collective entitlements to indigenous peoples living within their borders, such as rights to customary law, collective property and bilingual education.[11] So widespread and generalized was this shift that analysts such as Donna Lee Van Cott referred to a regional model of 'multicultural constitutionalism' (2000a) in Latin America. In effect what occurred was a multicultural reframing of individual rights and citizenship, with potentially far-reaching implications. Whereas previously citizenship had been conceived of in terms of individual entitlements and obligations, the new constitutional order meant that indigenous peoples were recognized as the collective subject of rights: indigenous people continued to be individual citizens, but indigenous *peoples* also acquired citizenship rights (Assies *et al.*, 1999; Sieder, 2002; Stavenhagen, 2002).

These constitutional reforms raised expectations that indigenous peoples' rights to political and legal autonomy would be respected by national governments and that policies would be implemented which would ensure respect for cultural difference and improved conditions for indigenous populations, who constitute the poorest and most marginalized of Latin America's citizens. Political scientist Deborah Yashar (2005) has signalled how the claims for indigenous rights which preceded the constitutional shift had their roots in the dismantling of corporate citizenship regimes and the neoliberal economic turn and associated reform of the state in different Latin American countries. While social movements of indigenous people mobilized to demand respect for cultural difference and an end to discrimination, their claims were also clearly material.

A range of policies were subsequently implemented by Latin American states and international development institutions to target indigenous people and promote 'development with identity' (Andolina *et al.*, 2009). Yet, by the twenty-first century, disillusionment and frustration set in as the limits of this multicultural policy model became evident. Inspired by the work of anthropologist Charles Hale, a number of authors developed sophisticated critiques of states' recognition of indigenous rights, signalling how neoliberal states can live with, indeed welcome cultural difference at the same time as they continue to implement macroeconomic policies which are destructive of indigenous livelihoods and life chances (Hale, 2002, 2006; Postero & Zamosc, 2004; Richards, 2004). Many rightly view at least the first wave of 'state-sponsored multiculturalism' (Postero, 2007, p. 13) as a mechanism to reconstitute the hegemony and legitimacy of weak states and fragile democracies, rather than signifying a real governmental commitment to guarantee rights for indigenous peoples. Despite the rhetorical commitment made to respecting indigenous rights implied by new constitutions and ratification of international instruments in Latin American counties, in case after case indigenous people continued to be persecuted by the state when they attempted to exercise their newly endorsed rights to autonomy and challenge hegemonic patterns of economic development. The targeted social policies developed during the 1990s were criticized as little more than tokenistic measures which provided limited paternalistic benefits. At the same time as more 'culturally appropriate' healthcare or educational provision was extended to indigenous populations, neoliberal economic development policies continued to threaten indigenous territories, despoil natural resources and displace indigenous peoples (Richards, 2004; Toledo Llancaqueo, 2005).[12] However, the fact that indigenous peoples' collective rights are now recognized as part of the block of constitutional norms in many countries has potentially opened up a new role for the judiciary in the defence of those rights. Perhaps just as importantly, the international legal commitments acquired by Latin American states towards their indigenous populations during the 1990s also raised the prospects of judicializing indigenous peoples' demands within a number of different arenas.

During the 1990s many states ratified the International Labour Organization's Convention 169 concerning Indigenous and Tribal Peoples in Independent Countries (ILO 169 hereafter). ILO 169 was approved by the ILO's General Assembly in 1989 and codifies the collective rights of indigenous and tribal peoples, setting out a series of obligations for state parties to the Convention. ILO 169 has been ratified by more states in Latin America than in any other region of the world. While processes of ratification have often been contentious, this regional endorsement signals the relative acceptance of the concept of indigenous peoples in Latin America, compared to Africa and Asia where the term is much more problematic. It can also be explained as part of the 'rights cascade' that followed the return to constitutional democracy throughout Latin America in the 1980s and 1990s, which involved the ratification of numerous human rights treaties by new democratically elected governments (Lutz & Sikkink, 2001). Latin American states parties to the ILO Convention include Argentina, Bolivia, Brazil, Chile, Colombia, Costa Rica, Ecuador, Honduras, Guatemala, Mexico, Peru, Paraguay and Venezuela.

Rights guaranteed by the Convention include equality of opportunity and treatment, protections for indigenous peoples' religion and spiritual values and customs, rights to ownership and possession of traditionally occupied lands, and rights to appropriate forms of health and education provision.[13] It also commits governments to recognizing the jurisdictional autonomy of indigenous peoples; articles 8, 9 and 10 of the Convention provide indigenous peoples with the right to administer their own forms of justice, as long as these respect fundamental and internationally recognized human rights.

In applying national laws and regulations to the peoples concerned, due regard shall be had to their customs or customary law. These peoples shall have the right to retain their own customs and institutions, where these are not incompatible with fundamental rights defined by the national legal system and with internationally recognized human rights. Procedures shall be established, wherever necessary, to resolve conflicts which may arise in the application of this principle.

(ILO 169, art. 8)

To the extent compatible with the national legal system and internationally recognized human rights, the methods customarily practiced by the peoples concerned for dealing with offences committed by their members shall be respected. The customs of these peoples in regard to penal matters shall be taken into consideration by the authorities and courts dealing with such cases.

(ILO 169, art. 9)

In imposing penalties laid down by general law on members of these peoples account shall be taken of their economic, social and cultural characteristics. Preference shall be given to methods of punishment other than confinement in prison.

(ILO 169, art. 10)

The Convention also specifies that indigenous peoples have a right to prior consultation on development proposals affecting their livelihoods.

In applying the provisions of this Convention, governments shall: consult the peoples concerned, through appropriate procedures and in particular through their representative institutions, whenever consideration is being given to legislative or administrative measures which may affect them directly.

(ILO 169, art. 6.1.a)

The peoples concerned shall have the right to decide their own priorities for the process of development as it affects their lives, beliefs, institutions and spiritual wellbeing and the lands they occupy or otherwise use, and to exercise control, to the extent possible, over their own economic, social and cultural development. In addition, they shall participate in the formulation, implementation and evaluation of plans and programs for national and regional development which may affect them directly.

(ILO 169, art. 7.1)

Governments shall ensure that, whenever appropriate, studies are carried out, in co-operation with the peoples concerned, to assess the social, spiritual, cultural and environmental impact on them of planned development activities. The results of these studies shall be considered as fundamental criteria for the implementation of these activities.

(ILO 169, art. 7.3)

In cases in which the State retains the ownership of mineral or sub-surface resources or rights to other resources pertaining to lands, governments shall establish or maintain procedures through which they shall consult these peoples, with a view to ascertaining whether and to what degree their interests would be prejudiced, before undertaking or permitting any programs for the exploration or exploitation of such resources pertaining to their lands. The peoples concerned shall wherever possible participate in the benefits of such activities, and shall receive fair compensation for any damages which they may sustain as a result of such activities.

(ILO 169, art. 15.2, emphasis added)

States in the region retain ownership of subsoil resources, but according to the principles of ILO 169 they cannot decide development priorities without prior consultation with the indigenous peoples who inhabit those territories. Disputes over the extent of indigenous autonomy and quite what is understood as adequate prior consultation have increasingly featured in domestic and regional courts in Latin America. This is partly because nowhere has prior consultation been defined through legislation in individual states. As I will discuss below with reference to the case of Guatemala, this lack of legal definition – involving commitment to a broad internationally sanctioned principle and lack of precision about how such principle should be upheld and made operational in practice – has prompted a range of different legal actions and engagements by indigenous people.

ILO 169 is the first international instrument dealing with indigenous peoples' rights that is binding on signatory states. However, it heralded part of a broader international trend towards codifying indigenous peoples and their rights within the international system. In September 2007 the UN General Assembly finally adopted the UN Declaration on the Rights of Indigenous People (UNDRIP), marking the culmination of more than twenty years of negotiations between states and indigenous peoples' representatives at the UN on the text of the declaration.[14] The Declaration recognizes the rights of indigenous peoples to the lands, territories and natural resources that are critical to their ways of life. Going much further than ILO 169, it affirms that indigenous peoples, like all peoples under international law, have the right to self-determination of which *free, prior and informed consent* is an integral part.[15]

(1) Indigenous peoples have the right to determine and develop priorities and strategies for the development or use of their lands or territories and other resources.
(2) States shall consult and cooperate in good faith with the indigenous peoples concerned through their own representative institutions in order to obtain their free and informed consent prior to the approval of any project affecting their lands or territories and other resources, particularly in connection with the development, utilization or exploitation of mineral, water or other resources.

(3) States shall provide effective mechanisms for just and fair redress for any such activities, and appropriate measures shall be taken to mitigate adverse environmental, economic, social, cultural or spiritual impact.

(UNDRIP, art. 32)

The UN Declaration is based upon principles of partnership, consultation and cooperation between indigenous peoples and states and reaffirms the international community's commitment to respect diversity and the right to difference. It is not legally binding because it has not yet achieved the status of a convention. However, by interpreting how existing international human rights law applies to indigenous peoples it sets new international standards for states to meet and constitutes the most complete statement to date of the international human rights of indigenous peoples. Irrespective of its non-binding character, it will become the new framework for all UN programmes and has already influenced the operating protocols of development NGOs and multilateral institutions such as the Inter-American Development Bank (see below). Bolivia was the first country in Latin America to adopt the UN Declaration on Indigenous Rights as national law, approving a National Law on Indigenous Peoples in November 2007 which is an exact copy of the declaration.

Negotiations continue on a proposed American Declaration on the Rights of Indigenous Peoples within the Organization of American States.[16] If that draft convention is finally approved and ratified by the requisite number of states it will become part of the regional norms enforceable through the Inter-American human rights system. However, even in the absence of a regional human rights instrument specifically addressing the collective rights of indigenous peoples, in the last decade indigenous peoples in the Americas have increasingly judicialized their claims at the regional level and even before UNDRIP's adoption by the General Assembly, the Inter-American Court of Human Rights had begun to cite the declaration in its rulings.[17] A number of contentious cases related to indigenous land claims and issues of prior consultation have been taken to the Inter-American Commission by indigenous movements and their allies. For example, in 1997 the U'wa people, in alliance with a number of Colombian and US-based NGOs, brought a case against the Colombian government to try to stop a mining concession in their territory granted to the Oxy and Shell oil companies, part of a long-running and multi-faceted legal battle between the U'wa and the Colombian state (Rodríguez-Garavito & Arenas, 2005). In 2001, in the celebrated case of Awas Tingni vs. Nicaragua, the Inter-American Court of Human Rights confirmed that indigenous peoples have collective rights not just to the land they occupy, but also to its resources. The judges declared that the rights of the indigenous community in question to territory and to judicial protection had been violated by the Nicaraguan government when it granted concessions to a Korean lumber company to log on their traditional land, and recommended a series of remedies.[18] Notwithstanding the fact that the implementation of the court's recommendations has been hugely contentious and complex,[19] this important and innovatory jurisprudence is a clear example of the ways in which social movements' engagement with law helps to shape international legal norms.

In addition to public international law comprising human rights instruments and the jurisprudence of the Inter-American Court, during the last two decades indigenous peoples and their rights and entitlements have also been encoded in the 'soft law' of international development institutions such as the World Bank, the Inter-American Development Bank and the various bilateral development agencies. This is part of the 'cultural turn' in international development practice (Radcliffe, 2006). In 1991 the World Bank issued its Operational Directive 4.20, which aimed to incorporate the principles of ILO 169 into World Bank operational guidelines and underlined the need for the 'informed participation' of indigenous people in development projects and plans affecting them (Davis, 2002). In 2005 the Bank replaced OP 4.20 with Operational Policy 4.10, which aimed to bring policy more in line with emerging principles of international law. In February 2006 the Inter-American Development Bank approved a comprehensive Operational Policy on Indigenous Peoples and Strategy for Indigenous Development, which entered into force in August 2006.[20] As well as providing a clear definition of indigenous peoples,[21] this policy also defines 'indigenous rights', 'indigenous governance' and 'development with identity', and commits the IDB to promoting 'development with identity' while protecting and safeguarding indigenous peoples' rights (Inter-American Development Bank, 2006). Like ILO 169, these internal norms establish the principle of prior consultation with indigenous peoples regarding development projects that directly affect them. It should be emphasized that these are internal guidelines within banks (which are accountable to their major shareholders), not norms which can be legally enforced in courts; any oversight mechanisms are internal to the banks themselves. Additionally, as with ILO 169, these guidelines fail to define precisely what constitutes adequate prior consultation. Both the World Bank and the Inter-American Development Bank have been strongly criticized for supporting large-scale investment projects to exploit natural resources that have been disastrous for indigenous livelihoods and the environment (Murray Li, 2007; Randeria, 2003; Sawyer, 2004). In this sense it is not at all clear that these new operational directives have made a significant difference to their overall lending practices (the IDB guidelines were only recently adopted, but the experience of the World Bank since the approval of operational directive 4.20 provides sufficient cause for scepticism). As the case from Guatemala examined below indicates, the incorporation of these kinds of internal norms or 'soft law' has provided additional possibilities for social movements to mobilize against prejudicial development interventions. Yet such legal mobilizations may risk ever more complex legal and quasi-legal entanglements, shaping indigenous political engagements yet offering limited concrete gains.

Guatemala: commitments to indigenous rights

In terms both of legal norms and public policy innovations, official multiculturalism in Guatemala is weak compared with other countries in the region, particularly the Andean countries where constitutional reforms recognizing indigenous rights and policy innovations aimed at providing 'development with identity' have been far-reaching. In Colombia, constitutional changes were a result of a crisis in governmental legitimacy (Van Cott, 2000a); in Ecuador and Bolivia they were the result of extensive organization and political mobilization by indigenous peoples (Lucero 2008; Yashar, 2005; Zamosc, 2004). In Guatemala the multiculturalization of the state was a consequence of the highly internationalized peace process, mediated by the UN, which was concluded in 1996, bringing an end to thirty-six years of armed conflict. Indigenous people had previously organized as part of the guerrilla movement or in human rights organizations. However, the massive violence of the military's counter-insurgent campaign, which left over 200,000 people assassinated or disappeared, severely limited the possibilities for mass-based popular movements to develop. Although Guatemala has one of the highest percentages of indigenous population in the Americas (approximately 50 per cent of the population are Mayan) and a long tradition of indigenous political organizing, it was not until the late 1980s that organizations emerged to specifically demand collective rights as indigenous peoples. Their demands were taken up within the peace process and amplified as a result. The government made a series of commitments to respect indigenous peoples' rights and identity. Following the signing of the final peace settlement, international development agencies and multilateral banks and donors took a leading role in supporting and implementing the agreements. As a consequence, the Guatemalan state was 'multiculturalized' to a significant degree, even though local elites tended to oppose the recognition of substantive rights for the indigenous population.

The Agreement on the Identity and Rights of Indigenous Peoples (AIDPI), signed by the government of Guatemala and the guerrillas of the Unidad Revolucionaria Nacional Guatemalteca (URNG) in May 1995, committed the Guatemalan state to implement a series of constitutional reforms in order to recognize indigenous peoples' collective rights.[22] These included the right to be subject to customary law, the right to bilingual education and protections for communally-held lands, but excluded territorially-based autonomy arrangements. After the final signing of the peace agreement in December 1996, indigenous organizations began to draft proposals for constitutional reform to recognize the collective rights of the indigenous population, including the right to select their own authorities and develop and apply their own forms of law within their communities. According to the terms of the peace agreement and the 1985 constitution itself, proposals for constitutional reform had to be first agreed by Congress and subsequently approved in a popular referendum. A package of constitutional reforms was finally approved in October 1998, nearly two years after the peace settlement was finalized, and covered an extensive range of issues, including reforms to the executive, judiciary and legislature. However, the recognition of indigenous rights was one of the most controversial aspects of the proposed reforms. Business elites mounted a vociferous campaign against the recognition of indigenous jurisdiction, fearing that recognizing indigenous rights to exercise law would inevitably raise the issue of territory and indigenous land claims. In the event, the proposed constitutional amendments were rejected in a national referendum on a turnout of just 18 per cent of the electorate.

In the absence of constitutional reform, the formal legal standing of indigenous rights is weak in Guatemala in contrast to, say, Colombia, Ecuador or Bolivia. Nonetheless, indigenous rights activists have looked to existing constitutional articles and to ILO 169 to support their rights claims. For example, two articles of the 1985 constitution provide a basis for recognizing indigenous authorities, their norms, procedures and decisions. Article 58 states that 'the right of people and communities to their cultural identity in accordance with their values, language and customs shall be recognized'. Article 66 states that: 'Guatemala is formed by diverse ethnic groups amongst whom are indigenous groups of Mayan descent. The state recognizes, respects and promotes their ways of life, customs, traditions, forms of social organization, use of indigenous dress by men and women, languages and dialects'. Some argue that 'recognizing, respecting and promoting' obligates state authorities to recognize the autonomy of indigenous authorities and their right to exercise customary law. However, this interpretation is not endorsed by the majority of high court judges in the country who tend to adhere to a more formalist and restrictive interpretation of the law.[23]

In addition to these constitutional articles, Guatemala ratified ILO Convention 169 on the rights of indigenous and tribal peoples in March 1995 and the Convention finally entered into force in the country in June 1997. A number of attempts were made within and outside the legislature to block its adoption, but its adoption was strongly supported by the UN and major international donors supporting the peace process. A consultative opinion of the Guatemalan Constitutional Court requested at the time of ratification concluded that Convention 169 did not contradict the Guatemalan constitution.[24] Some jurists argue that article 46 of the constitution, which gives international human rights conventions and treaties ratified by Guatemala pre-eminence over domestic law, means that, in effect, ILO 169 is superior to internal legislation. However, there is no clear policy on the part of the Guatemalan Supreme Court, Constitutional Court or head of the public prosecution service (*Fiscal General*) with respect to the application of ILO Convention 169 or indeed the legal implications of articles 58 and 66 of the constitution. Many lawyers tend to view constitutional articles and international conventions as abstract statements of principle rather than judiciable rights, arguing that secondary legislation is required to make the principles into binding law. The status of ILO 169 then remains highly contested.

Sipakapa: challenging the logic of neoliberal development through law

In recent years conflicts between indigenous peoples' views about development and state-endorsed investment practices have become acute in Guatemala, as they have in many regions of Latin America. As part of economic liberalization reforms, a new Mining Code was approved in 1997 (Decree no. 48–97). This law reversed previous restrictions on foreign companies owning 100 per cent of mining operations, increased tax breaks and investment opportunities for transnational capital and reduced the royalties payable to the Guatemalan state to just 1 per cent. This law is part of a global trend of legal reforms which are part and parcel of the neoliberal development model – some campaigners estimate that over seventy countries have 'modernized' their mining legislation in recent years.[25] In line with the new legislation, a significant number of licences for mineral, hydroelectric and oil exploitation were extended to domestic and foreign companies. This was part of an accelerated expansion of investment in natural resource exploitation which has occurred throughout the region since the early 1990s, driven by rising commodity prices and accompanied by complex processes of international financing. While these mining companies are registered in particular countries, they are subject to frequent mergers and acquisitions and operate through many different local subsidiaries, making it hard to keep track of precisely which economic interests are behind particular projects and where efforts to ensure greater accountability can be directed.

As a consequence of these new policies towards transnational capital, mining operations have begun in different sites throughout Guatemala, many of them in areas of high indigenous residence and extreme poverty. As mentioned above, indigenous peoples have no legal rights to territorial autonomy in Guatemala and – in common with the rest of Latin America – states retain the rights to subsoil resources. However, ILO 169, together with the 'soft law' of the World Bank, IDB and other donors, clearly points to a requirement for prior consultation about development projects which will affect indigenous peoples' ways of life. Yet in Guatemala, as elsewhere in the region, no regulatory framework to mediate the interests of private capital and the collective rights of indigenous peoples has been established. In his study of mining operations in indigenous areas of Peru, David Szablowski has observed that state support for mining development relies on a 'strategy of selective absence' whereby states effectively delegate the 'responsibility for the social mediation of mining development' to the mining companies (2007, p. 58). In a context characterized by extreme poverty, ethnic discrimination, chronic mistrust on the part of indigenous communities towards government and suspicions of the motives and methods of transnational corporations, and continued state and para-statal violence, the prospect of effective and peaceful mediation by international companies is extremely low.

During the decade and a half since the peace accords were concluded, domestic and international NGOs and UN agencies working in Guatemala have worked to promote indigenous 'rights consciousness' and to strengthen local forms of indigenous organization. In 2004 and 2005 indigenous community activists in the western department of San Marcos mobilized to call on the government to annul a concession for open-cast gold and silver mining and processing, known as the Marlin project. The license for exploration was granted to Montana Exploradora SA, a subsidiary of Canadian mining company Glamis Gold, in 1996, the first mining project to be approved according to the new 1997 Mining Code. The project was supported by the World Bank, receiving some $35 million in loans and $10 million in equity investment from the International Financial Corporation, the branch of the World Bank which lends to private companies (Fulmer *et al.*, 2008; Solano, 2005). Although the licence was approved after the national congress had ratified ILO Convention 169, the indigenous Maya Mam and Sipakapense communities of the directly affected municipalities of San Miguel Ixtahuacán and Sipakapa were not consulted about the proposed mining project. The company began operations in San Marcos in 2004 and local protests soon gathered pace, drawing support from environmentalists, the Catholic Church and indigenous and popular organizations in other parts of the country. In January 2005 an indigenous protestor was killed when police opened fire on a demonstration in the neighbouring department of Sololá attempting to block the passage of mining equipment to San Marcos along the Panamerican highway. Sixteen indigenous activists, including the mayor of Sololá, were subsequently charged with terrorism (Solano, 2005).

The issue of adequate prior consultation was effectively put to the test in a protracted contest between Montana Exploradora and local activists. When Glamis applied to the World Bank's International Financial Corporation for support for the Marlin project, it had to organize consultations as a re-quirement to receive the loan. The company claimed it had spoken to around 3000 people in San Marcos. However, many of those supposedly consulted subsequently claimed that in fact company representatives had merely presented the mine as a *fait accompli* or 'done deal'. They alleged they had been given little information about the environmental and health impacts it might have, including those related to possible cyanide contamination of the water table. They also claimed that at no point did the company representatives give them an opportunity to make any decisions about the project. Predictably, the Marlin project was denounced as an anti-democratic imposition and demands grew for development priorities for the municipality and surrounding areas to be decided by local people.

In June 2005 a public consultation was announced by the municipal authorities of Sipakapa. This was to be held via open community assemblies in different villages. Montana Exploradora immediately tried to impede the vote, submitting a legal injunction to order the municipality to suspend proceedings. In the end pressure from the company forced the municipal mayor to back down. However, the local Community Development Council, a body set up as part of the ongoing process of municipal decentralization, held the consultation regardless. The 2002 legislation establishing rural and urban community development councils and the 2002 Municipal Code clearly state that the councils can convene plebiscites on matters of local concern affecting the rights and interests of indigenous communities at the request of indigenous authorities or communities, and that they will respect local indigenous principles, norms, procedures and forms of authority, including the community assembly.[26] In all, eleven out of thirteen villages voted against the mining development, mostly unanimously. The Ministry of Energy and Mines submitted an injunction to the Constitutional Court claiming that the popular vote was unconstitutional. However, the court upheld the villagers' right to organize a plebiscite and vote, citing ILO Convention 169 and the 2002 municipal code. However, the court failed to comment on the substance of the ballot itself: the communities in question had effectively rejected the mining operations, voting in favour or against the Marlin project in the community assemblies. Yet ILO 169, which partly inspired this quasi-legal mobilization, does not provide indigenous peoples with a right of veto. It merely affirms their rights to prior consultation and to the benefits of such development operations. When communities reject development initiatives such as the Marlin mine the Convention provides little guidance about how such conflicts can be resolved.

The Sipakapa consultation was the first time that an exercise of this type was held in Guatemala invoking ILO 169 to contest mining operations. In addition, a series of legal and quasi-legal or 'soft law' actions against the Marlin mining concession were filed outside the country by Guatemalan popular organizations and NGOs, evidencing the transnationalization of indigenous rights claims. UNISTRAGUA, a trade union confederation, filed a complaint with the ILO itself, alleging that the government had failed to meet its obligations to ensure due consultation. In addition, Madre Selva, a local environmental NGO, together with community representatives from Sipakapa, filed a complaint with the Compliance Advisory Ombudsman, the office that investigates complaints against projects funded by the World Bank's International Financial Corporation.[27] In August 2005 the World Bank's Compliance Advisory Ombudsman issued a report stating that the bank had failed to consult the local community adequately or properly evaluate the environmental and humanitarian impact of the mine.[28] The report also noted that regulations applying to mining operations in Guatemala provided no guidance on how companies should seek approval from local people for their activities. NGO activists also presented a case against the state of Guatemala before the Inter-American Commission of Human Rights in the hope that the case would eventually be heard in the Inter-American Court of Human Rights.

These legal and quasi-legal engagements by indigenous social movements and their allies represent new developments in indigenous peoples' fight to defend their natural resources and territories. Subsequent to the Sipakapa poll, other indigenous communities organized similar consultation processes in opposition to proposals for natural resource exploitation. Yet the results of these different legal and quasi-legal engagements have been far from encouraging. NGOs and the mining companies have battled over the relative rights of indigenous peoples and mining companies in the Guatemalan courts. A major victory was achieved by campaigners in April 2007 when the Constitutional Court upheld an appeal against the 1997 Mining Law presented by the Centre for Legal, Environmental and Social Action (CALAS). However, the court's objections to the Mining Law were primarily on environmental grounds (Central America Report, 27 June 2008). On the more vexed issue of prior consultation rights for indigenous peoples, the court ruled in favour of an appeal put forward by Montana Exploradora claiming that the Sipakapa plebiscite was unconstitutional. The court's view was that such popular consultations had no basis in law and that the municipal authorities of Sipakapa had no right to forbid Montana from operating in the area, as only the Ministry of Energy and Mines could decide energy policies (Central America Report, 1 June 2007). The court's ruling points to the central weakness of ILO 169: while prior consultation must be ensured, its outcomes are not legally binding. Mining companies – and therefore the signatory governments that endorse their operations – can remain within the legal obligations set out by the Convention merely by ensuring that communities are informed about future developments. Unlike the 2007 UN Declaration on the Rights of Indigenous People, which stipulates that 'free, informed and prior consent' must be obtained, ILO 169 does not imply any rights of voice, much less veto, on the part of indigenous communities residing on the lands where such operations are carried out. Such partial recognition of rights, and the accompanying legal fragmentation characteristic of globalization, may result in long and exhausting legal engagements on the part of social movements without any guarantee of longer-term benefits. Despite attempts by indigenous organizations in Guatemala during 2008 and 2009 to promote legislation to regulate prior consultation, no new law has been approved by congress. Meanwhile construction of the mine and plant for cyanide processing of the ore at Sipakapa has continued, together with threats and intimidation against local activists who oppose the plant.

Conclusions

By juxtaposing the now internationally sanctioned collective human rights of indigenous peoples and the failure of governments to deliver on those rights in practice, indigenous peoples' movements have framed a powerful critique of hegemonic forms of development and globalization. They have increasingly challenged liberal conceptions of rights premised on ideas of property as something which can be assigned a monetary value and allocated to, or bought by individuals, irrespective of their connection to a specific place. And in their demands for greater recognition of political autonomy rights they also call into question and destabilize established understandings of democracy and citizenship as a contract between individuals and government alone. Yet such challenges take place within an increasingly complex and fragmented panorama of globalized legal pluralism, where the promises contained within international charters of indigenous peoples' rights are often directly at odds with international and national legal regimes governing trade and investment.

Balakrishnan Rajagopal underlines the regulatory and emancipatory tensions of law when he writes that 'human rights discourse ... is now not only the language of resistance, but also that of governance' (2003, p. 168). I have suggested here that the legal recognition of indigenous peoples' rights by states and the international community has provided opportunities and risks for social movements. The codification of rights in legal instruments provides avenues for new forms of struggle and engagement. However, by its very nature such codification also determines certain categories – such as 'prior consultation' – which become the focus of legal dispute, risking the possibility that complex political and cultural struggles get reduced to highly technical debates over legal definitions. In Colombia the U'wa people fought a complex legal battle against oil exploration in their territories for more than fifteen years, involving complaints before the Colombian Supreme Court, the Constitutional Court and the Inter-American Commission of Human Rights. In each case, the key issue was whether the government had undertaken adequate consultation with indigenous communities prior to granting licenses for exploration. In the face of continued protests by U'wa groups, in January 2006 a decision by the Council of State (*Consejo de Estado*) held that the government had met its legal obligations with respect to prior consultation, that the lack of agreement between the government and the affected communities and the latter's refusal to take part in a consultation process did not affect the legality of the initiation of oil exploration.[29] Independently of the outcome of legal petitions, sectors of the U'wa continue to argue for a radically different vision of development. However, their experience of legal mobilization points to the difficulty of securing accountability and effective voice through actions before domestic and international courts.

The increasingly plural legal landscape associated with contemporary globalization has generated powerful new forms of regulation (including state-endorsed multiculturalism), but has also opened up new possibilities for counter-hegemonic struggles. However, ultimately state sovereignty is increasingly fragmented and the locus of legal and political responsibility – where the buck stops – far from clear. Creative engagements with the principle of collective rights for indigenous peoples enshrined in ILO 169 and at least partially endorsed by multicultural constitutional reforms across Latin America are generating new forms of political action that press governments to make good on their promises. But, at the same time, given their failure to guarantee those rights in practice, this has led to increased levels of confrontation between indigenous peoples, government agencies and transnational corporations. In the fragmented sovereignties and legalities of contemporary states, legal recognition of rights for distinct cultural groups such as indigenous peoples has gone hand in hand with new forms of capital accumulation, violence and exclusion. As John and Jean Comaroff have observed, in many postcolonial states 'the reach of the state is uneven and the landscape is a palimpsest of contested sovereignties, codes and jurisdictions' (2006, p. 9). At the same time 'vastly lucrative returns ... inhere in actively sustaining zones of ambiguity between the presence and absence of the law' (2006, p. 5). The ever expanding opportunities for legal engagement generated by the codification of indigenous rights may also, ultimately, contribute to sustaining such forms of ambiguity and profit at the same time as it opens possibilities for new counter-hegemonic politics.

Acknowledgements

An earlier version of this paper was presented at the workshop 'Governing Cultures? Neoliberalism, Democracy and the Question of Diversity', held at the University of Manchester, 26–7 March 2007. I am grateful to all the participants for their helpful comments and particularly to the two anonymous reviewers of *Economy and Society* for their suggestions.

Notes

1 The role of NGOs and civil society organizations in driving this global 'rights revolution' has been fundamental. As Douglas Cassel has observed, it would be wrong to view human rights law as an autonomous set of norms and institutions – 'without constant advocacy and agitation from NGOs, human rights treaties would not be drafted or ratified, enforcement mechanisms not created or used, and violators not constantly exposed' (Cassel, 2004, p. 20).
2 The Centro de Estudios Legales (CELS) in Argentina or DeJusticia in Colombia, for example, are trailblazers in advancing collective rights entitlements through public action litigation in Latin America.
3 For discussions of recent experiences of judicialization in Latin America and other new democracies, see Gargarella *et al.* (2006), Gloppen *et al.* (2004), Santos (2002), Sieder *et al.* (2005) and Couso *et al.* (2010).
4 On the transnationalization of legal fields, see Trubek *et al.* (1994).
5 Effectively foreign investors now have the right to file suit against laws or regulations at the national, state or local levels if they consider these may result in a breach of contract, even if these laws or regulations are enacted for public interest objectives, such as environmental protection or public health.

6 International commercial arbitration is often referred to as a kind of 'soft law' because of its apparently voluntary nature (the parties to a contract have to agree to be bound by such terms). Its growth has seemed to suggest to some that the law of nation-states is becoming increasingly irrelevant to international commercial transactions and the functioning of the global economy. Contracts are made between private entities and are increasingly regulated outside national legal systems and courts. However, a more sceptical view of this kind of legal globalization – while recognizing the importance and impact of these new transnational legal phenomena – would argue that state law continues to be central to global economic production and regulation. As Eve Darian-Smith observes, 'state sovereignty and state law *have* been important in sustaining, servicing, and enforcing global economic operations, and *will remain so* in the foreseeable future' (2000, p. 811).

7 As Randeria (2003, p. 320) underlines, the World Bank inspection panel ostensibly functions to review the extent to which bank staff have met the procedures and rules of the institution; it does not adjudicate between parties to a conflict.

8 Recent anthropological engagements with the state suggest that such apparent 'lawlessness' is not so much about the absence of the state; rather, it constitutes a defining characteristic of 'stateness'. The bibliography is extensive, but see Das and Poole (2004), Comaroff and Comaroff (2006) and Hansen and Stepputat (2001, 2005) for useful discussions.

9 It is analytically insufficient to juxtapose 'legal' state behaviour against illegal, non-state actions: the legal and the illegal exist in a constant interplay and indeed are constitutive of the very nature of law. See Veena Das and Deborah Poole (2004) on the Janus-faced nature of the state and its 'illegibility'.

10 In their analysis of 'subaltern cosmopolitan legality', Boaventura de Sousa Santos and César Rodríguez-Garavito emphasize three points: first, the fact that 'experiments in subaltern cosmopolitan legality ... seek to articulate new notions of rights that go beyond the liberal ideal of individual autonomy, and incorporate solidaristic under-standings of entitlements grounded on alternative forms of legal knowledge' (2005, p. 16). Second, they argue against fetishizing the law, stressing the need to see counter-hegemonic legal actions as part of broader political struggles. And, third, they em-phasize the multi-scale nature of such 'subaltern cosmopolitan legality', pointing to the ways in which social movements 'exploit the opportunities offered by an increasingly plural legal landscape' (2005, p. 16).

11 A detailed comparison of these reforms is beyond the scope of this paper. The nature and extent of the constitutional rights extended to indigenous peoples through this first round of 'multicultural reforms' continues to be a matter of controversy across the region. For an earlier overview, see Van Cott (2000b).

12 Richards examines the case of Chile – one of the few Latin American countries not to have reformed its constitution to recognize indigenous rights. Chile was also one of the last countries in the region to ratify ILO Convention 169, which was finally approved by President Bachelet in September 2008, following approval by the Chilean Senate.

13 See http://www.unhchr.ch/html/menu3/b/62.htm (accessed 4 January 2010).

14 The UN General Assembly approved the Draft Declaration with 143 states voting in favour. Only four countries voted against adoption – Canada, Australia, New Zealand and the United States – and eleven states abstained (Azerbaijan, Bangladesh, Bhutan, Burundi, Columbia, Georgia, Kenya, Nigeria, the Russian Federation, Samoa and Ukraine).

15 The UN Declaration, by codifying 'free, prior and informed consent', provides a much stronger instrument than ILO Convention 169, which merely affirms the right to 'prior consultation' – a much more ambiguous term.

16 OEA/Ser/L/V/.II.95 Doc. 6 (1997).

17 The Inter-American Commission and Court uphold the instruments of the Inter-American system (the Declaration and the Convention), but also have a mandate to ensure respect for all human rights treaties ratified by member states – such as ILO 169.

18 An extensive bibliography exists about this case. See particularly Nash Rojas (2004), Rodríguez-Pinero Royo (2004) and Anaya and Crider (1996).

19 See comments by James Anaya, United Nations Special Rapporteur on the situation of human rights and fundamental freedoms of indigenous people, in 'Anaya: Nicaragua's titling of communal lands marks major step for indigenous rights', http:// www.galdu.org/web/index.php?odas = 3577&giella1 = eng (accessed 4 January 2010).

20 This document can be found at http://www.iadb.org/sds/IND/site_401_e.htm (accessed 4 January 2010).

21 'For the purposes of this policy, the term *indigenous peoples* refers to those who meet the following three criteria: (i) they are descendants from populations inhabiting Latin America and the Caribbean at the time of the conquest or colonization; (ii) irrespective of their legal status or current residence, they retain some or all of their own social, economic, political, linguistic and cultural institutions and practices; and (iii) they recognize themselves as belonging to indigenous or pre-colonial cultures or peoples.'

22 Guatemala's majority indigenous population who constitute the poorest and most marginalized sector of the population. According to World Bank figures for 2000, while Guatemala's twenty-three indigenous groups represented 43 per cent of the population (a conservative estimate), they accounted for 58 per cent of the poor and 72 per cent of the extremely poor. Almost three-quarters of indigenous people live in poverty, as compared with 41 per cent for non-indigenous (World Bank, 2003, p. 4).

23 In contrast to high courts in other Latin American countries, neither Guatemala's Supreme Court nor its Constitutional Court (created in 1986) has developed a proactive, rights-enforcing jurisprudence. On the role of high courts in 'rights revolutions', see the essays in Sieder *et al.* (2005) and Couso et al. (2010).

24 In its opinion the court stated that no incompatibility existed between the 1985 constitution and Convention 169. Constitutional Court of Guatemala, case file 199-95.

25 Rights Action (2005: 9).

26 Ley de Consejos de Desarrollo Urbano y Rural, article 15; Código Municipal, article 65.

27 For a discussion of mining and the World Bank, see Szablowski (2007); for a more detailed discussion of the Sipakapa complaint before the Compliance Advisory Ombudsman, see Fulmer *et al.* (2008).

28 See Compliance Advisory Ombudsman (2005).

29 For full text of the decision, see http://www.ramajudicial.gov.co/csj_portal/ assets/consejoestado/1708.htm (accessed 4 January 2010).

References

Anaya, S. J. & Crider, T. (1996). Indigenous peoples, the environment and commercial forestry in developing countries: The case of Awas Tingni, Nicaragua. *Human Rights Quarterly, 18*, 345–67.

Andolina, R., Laurie, N. & Radcliffe, S. (2009). *Indigenous development in the Andes: Culture, power and transnationalism.* Durham, NC: Duke University Press.

Assies, W., Hoekema, A. & Van der Haar, G. (1999). *The challenge of diversity: Indigenous peoples and reform of the state in Latin America.* Amsterdam: Thela.

Cassel, D. (2004). The globalization of human rights: consciousness, law and reality.

Northwestern University Journal of International Human Rights, 2(6).

Comaroff, J. L. & Comaroff, J. (Eds.) (2006). *Law and disorder in the postcolony.* Chicago, IL, and London: University of Chicago Press.

Compliance Advisory Ombudsman. (2005). *Assessment of a complaint submitted to CAO in relation to the Marlin Mining Project in Guatemala.* Office of the Compliance Advisory Ombudsman International Finance Corporation/ Multilateral Investment Guarantee Agency.

Couso, J., Huneeus, A. & Sieder, R. (Eds.) (2009). *Cultures of legality: Judicialization and political activism in Latin America.* Cambridge and New York: Cambridge University Press.

Darian-Smith, E. (2000). Review essay: Structural inequalities in the global legal system. *Law and Society Review, 34*(3), 809–28.

Das, V. & Poole, D. (Eds.) (2004). *Anthropology in the margins of the state.* Santa Fe, NM, and Oxford: School of American Research Press.

Davis, S. (2002). Indigenous peoples, poverty and participatory development: The experience of the World Bank in Latin America. In R. Sieder (Ed.), *Multiculturalism in Latin America: Indigenous rights, diversity and democracy* (pp. 227–51). Basingstoke and London: Palgrave.

Dezalay, Y. & Garth, B. G. (1996). *Dealing in virtue: International commercial arbitration and the construction of a transnational legal order.* Chicago, IL, and London: University of Chicago Press.

Friedman, L. M. (2002). One world: Notes on the emerging legal order. In M. Likosky (Ed.), *Transnational legal processes: Globalisation and power disparities* (pp. 23–40). London: Butterworths/LexisNexis.

Fulmer, A. M., Snodgrass Godoy, A. & Neff, P. (2008). Indigenous rights, resistance, and the law: Lessons from a Guatemalan mine. *Latin American Politics and Society, 50*(4), 91–121.

Gargarella, R., Domingo, P. & Roux, T. (Eds.) (2006). *Courts and social transformation in new democracies: An institutional voice for the poor?* Aldershot: Ashgate.

Geertz, C. (1993). Fact and law in comparative perspective. In *Local knowledge: Further essays in interpretive anthropology* (2nd ed., pp. 167–234). London: Fontana.

Gloppen, S., Gargarella, R. & Sklaar, E. (Eds.) (2004). *Democratization and the judiciary: The accountability function of courts in new democracies.* London and Portland, OR: Frank Cass.

Goodale, M. & Merry, S. E. (Eds.) (2007). *The practice of human rights: Tracking law between the global and the local.* Cambridge and New York: Cambridge University Press.

Hale, C. R. (2002). Does multiculturalism menace? Governance, cultural rights and the politics of identity in Guatemala. *Journal of Latin American Studies, 34*, 485–524.

Hale, C. R. (2006). *Más que un indio: Racial ambivalence and neoliberal multiculturalism in Guatemala.* Santa Fe, NM, and Oxford: School of American Research Press.

Hansen, T. B. & Stepputat, F. (Eds.) (2001). *States of imagination: Ethnographic explorations of the post-colonial state.* Durham, NC: Duke University Press.

Hansen, T. B. & Stepputat, F. (Eds.) (2005). *Sovereign bodies: Citizens, migrants and states in the postcolonial world.* Princeton, NJ, and Oxford: Princeton University Press.

Inter-American Development Bank. (2006). *Operational policy on indigenous peoples and strategy for indigenous development.* Retrieved January 2010 from http://idbdocs.iadb.org/wsdocs/ getdocument.aspx?docnum =2032081.

Keck, M. & Sikkink, K. (1998). *Activists beyond borders: Advocacy networks in international politics.* Ithaca, NY: Cornell University Press.

Lucero, J. A. (2008). *Struggles of voice: The politics of indigenous representation in the Andes.* Pittsburgh, PA: University of Pittsburgh Press.

Lutz, E. & Sikkink, K. (2001). The justice cascade: The evolution and impact of human rights trials in Latin America.

Chicago Journal of International Law, 2,
1–33.

Merry, S. E. (2001). Rights, religion and community: Approaches to violence against women in the context of globalization. *Law and Society Review, 35*(1), 39–88.

Merry, S. E. (2004). Constructing a global law: Violence against women and the human rights system. *Law and Social Inquiry, 28*(4), 941–77.

Merry, S. E. (2006). *Human rights and gender violence: translating international law into local justice.* Chicago, IL, and London: University of Chicago Press.

Morgan, R. (2004a). Advancing indigenous rights at the United Nations. PhD thesis, University of Essex.

Morgan, R. (2004b). Advancing indigenous rights at the United Nations: Strategic framing and its impact on the normative development of international law. *Social and Legal Studies, 13*(4), 481–500.

Morgan, R. (2007). On political institutions and social movement dynamics: The case of the United Nations and the global indigenous movement. *International Political Science Review, 28*(3), 273–92.

Murray Li, T. (2007). *The will to improve: Governmentality, development, and the practice of politics.* Durham, NC: Duke University Press.

Nash Rojas, C. (2004). Los derechos humanos de los indígenas en la jurisprudencia de la Corte Interamericana de Derechos Humanos. In J. Aylwin (Ed.), *Derechos humanos y pueblos indígenas: Tendencias internacionales y contexto Chileno* (pp. 29–43). Temuco: Instituto de Estudios Indígenas/Universidad de la Frontera.

O'Donnell, G. (1993). On the state, democratisation and some conceptual problems: A Latin American view with glances at some post-communist countries. *World Development, 21*(8), 1355–71.

Postero, N. G. (2007). *Now we are citizens: Indigenous politics in postmulticultural Bolivia.* Stanford, CA: Stanford University Press.

Postero, N. G. & Zamosc, L. (Eds.) (2004). *The struggle for indigenous rights in Latin America.* Brighton and Portland, OR: Sussex Academic Press.

Radcliffe, S. (2006). Culture in development thinking: Geographies, actors, and paradigms. In S. Radcliffe (Ed.), *Culture and development in a globalizing world: Geographies, actors and paradigms.* London and New York: Routledge.

Rajagopal, B. (2003). *International law from below: Development, social movements and third world resistance.* Cambridge and New York: Cambridge University Press.

Randeria, S. (2003). Glocalization of law: Environmental justice, World Bank, NGOs and the cunning state in India. *Current Sociology, 51*(3–4), 305–28.

Richards, P. (2004). *Pobladores, indígenas and the state.* Piscataway, NJ: Rutgers University Press.

Rights Action. (2005). A backwards, upside-down kind of development: Global actors, mining and community-based resistance in Honduras and Guatemala. Retrieved 26 October 2008 from http://www.rightsaction.org/Reports/Cuffe%20mining%20report%202005–03.htm.

Risse, T., Ropp, S. C. & Sikkink, K. (Eds.) (1999). *The power of human rights: International norms and domestic politics* (pp. 1–38). Cambridge: Cambridge University Press.

Rodgers, D. (2006). The state as gang: Conceptualizing the governmentality of violence in Nicaragua. *Critique of Anthropology, 26*(3), 315–30.

Rodríguez-Garavito, C. & Arenas, L. C. (2005). Indigenous rights, transnational activism, and legal mobilization: The struggle of the U'wa people in Colombia. In B. de S. Santos & C. Rodríguez-Garavito (Eds.), *Law and globalization from below: Towards a cosmopolitan legality* (pp. 241–66). Cambridge and New York: Cambridge University Press.

Rodríguez-Pinero Royo, L. (2004). El caso Awas Tingni y el régimen de derechos territoriales indígenas en la Costa Atlántica de Nicaragua. In José Aylwin (Ed.), *Derechos humanos y pueblos indígenas: Tendencias* *internacionales y contexto chileno* (pp. 218–33). Temuco, Instituto de Estudios Indígenas/Universidad de la Frontera.

Salvatore, R. D., Aguirre, C. & Joseph, G. M. (Eds.) (2001). *Crime and punishment in Latin America: Law and society since late colonial times.* Durham, NC, and London: Duke University Press.

Santamaría, Á. (2008). *Redes transnacionales y emergencia de la diplomacia indígena: Un estudio del caso colombiano.* Bogotá: Editorial Universidad del Rosario.

Santos, B. de S. (1998). *La globalización del derecho: Los nuevos caminos de la regulación y la emancipación.* Colombia: ILSA.

Santos, B. de S. (2002). *Toward a new legal common sense* (2nd ed.). London: Butterworths/LexisNexis.

Santos, B. de S. & Rodríguez-Garavito, C. (2005). Law, politics and the subaltern in counter-hegemonic globalization. In B. de S. Santos & C. Rodríguez-Garavito (Eds.), *Law and globalization from below: Towards a cosmopolitan legality* (pp. 1–26). Cambridge and New York: Cambridge University Press.

Sawyer, S. (2004). *Crude chronicles: Indigenous politics, multinational oil, and neoliberalism in Ecuador.* Durham, NC: Duke University Press.

Sieder, R. (Ed.) (2002). *Multiculturalism in Latin America: Indigenous rights, diversity and democracy.* Basingstoke and London: Palgrave.

Sieder, R. & Witchell, J. (2001). Advancing indigenous claims through the law: Reflections on the Guatemalan peace process. In J. Cowan, M. Dembour & R. Wilson (Eds.), *Culture and rights* (pp. 201–25). Cambridge: Cambridge University Press.

Sieder, R., Schjolden, L. & Angell, A. (Eds.) (2005). *The judicialization of politics in Latin America.* New York: Palgrave.

Sikkink, K. (2005). The transnational dimension of the judicialization of politics in Latin America. In R. Sieder, L. Schjolden & A. Angell (Eds.), *The judicialization of politics in Latin America* (pp. 263–92). New York: Palgrave.

Solano, L. (2005). *Guatemala petróleo y minería en las entrañas del poder.* Guatemala City: Inforpress Centroamericana.

Starr, J. & Goodale, M. (2003). *Practicing ethnography in law: New dialogues, enduring methods.* New York: Palgrave Macmillan.

Stavenhagen, R. (2002). Indigenous peoples and the state in Latin America: An ongoing debate. In R. Sieder (Ed.), *Multiculturalism in Latin America: Indigenous rights, diversity and democracy* (pp. 24–44). Basingstoke and London: Palgrave.

Stephen, L. (2005). Negotiating global, national, and local 'rights' in a Zapotec community. *PoLAR Political and Legal Anthropology Review, 28*(1), 133–50.

Szablowski, D. (2007). *Transnational law and local struggles: Mining communities and the World Bank.* Oxford and Portland, OR: Hart Publishing.

Tate, C. N. & Vallinder, Y. (Eds.) (1995). *The global expansion of judicial power.* New York: New York University Press.

Teubner, G. (Ed.) (1997). *Global law without a state.* Aldershot: Dartmouth.

Toledo Llancaqueo, V. (2005). Políticas indígenas y derechos territoriales en América Latina: 1990–2004: ¿Las fronteras indígenas de la globalización? In P. Dávalos (Comp.), *Pueblos indígenas: Estado y democracia* (pp. 67–102). Buenos Aires: CLACSO.

Trubek, D. M., Dezalay, Y., Buchanan, R. & Davis., J. R. (1994). Global restructuring and the law: Studies of the internationalization of legal fields and the creation of transnational arenas. *Case Western Reserve Law Review, 44*, 407–98.

Twining, W. (2000). *Globalisation and legal theory.* Evanston, IL: Northwestern University Press.

Van Cott, D. L. (2000a). *The friendly liquidation of the past: The politics of diversity in Latin America.* Pittsburgh, PA: Pittsburgh University Press.

Van Cott, D. L. (2000b). Latin America: Constitutional reform and ethnic rights. *Parliamentary Affairs, 53*, 41–54.

Wilson, R. (Ed.) (1997). *Human rights, culture and context: Anthropological perspectives on human rights*. London: Pluto Press.

Wilson, R. (2000). Reconciliation and revenge in post-apartheid South Africa: Rethinking human rights and legal pluralism. *Current Anthropology, 41*(1), 75–98.

World Bank. (2003). *Guapa: Guatemala poverty assessment*. Guatemala: World Bank.

Yashar, D. (2005). *Contesting citizenship in Latin America: The rise of indigenous movements and the postliberal challenge*. Cambridge: Cambridge University Press.

Zamosc, L. (2004). The Indian movement in Ecuador: From politics of influence to politics of power. In N. G. Postero & L. Zamosc (Eds.), *The struggle for indigenous rights in Latin America* (pp. 131–57). Brighton and Portland, OR: Sussex Academic Press.

The law cuts both ways: rural legal activism and citizenship struggles in neosocialist China

Susanne Brandtstädter

Abstract

This paper will draw on fieldwork in rural China and other sources to explore the interrelations between 'governing culture' and the question of 'participation and equal rights' as they reveal themselves in struggles over 'the rule of law' in contemporary China. As around the globe, the opening up to the global market and the construction of a modern legal system led in China to a new identity politics and a foregrounding of cultural citizenship as an arena of governance and a political struggle for rights. My interest is here the interrelation between a 'civilizing' project of the neosocialist state to create law-abiding, formally equal citizens, and a new, self-propelled law activism among Chinese 'peasants' who seek to appropriate the law not just to defend themselves against the infringements of local governments on their 'civil rights' or even 'human rights', but to recreate themselves as peasants, citizens and political subjects, as new subjects for rights. I will argue that such citizenship struggles can be explored only with reference to the historical formation of governance in a given place; in this case with reference to Maoism, its political split between peasants and urbanites, and a particular formulation of citizenship that I call 'transcendental'.

Introduction

The era of 'Reform and Opening Up', as the post-Maoist period in China is officially called, has been defined through three movements that constitute formal hallmarks of liberalism: a movement, within the economic sphere, towards privatization and the market; within the political sphere, towards the rule of law; and, within the social or cultural sphere, towards a 'civil' society of self-regulating, entrepreneurial individuals. Historically these movements find their precedents in ideas of radical elites during the first Chinese republic (1912–49), a time when the first steps towards a modern legal system were taken, and when new terms such as science (*kexue*), democracy (*minzhu*), republic (*gonghe*), law (*falü*), rights (*quanli*) and individual (*geren*) entered the political vocabulary. But only the conjuncture of the post-Maoist state with a global neoliberal agenda and the global market after 1980 allowed these 'movements' to affect the social relations and personal desires of Chinese people in an unprecedented way, also recasting the parameters of citizenship in China – in the legal-political, as well as the social-cultural dimensions of the term (Fong & Murphy, 2006; Zhang & Ong, 2008). Of at least equal importance to understand post-Maoist governance, and thus the nature of citizenship, however, remains the state's Maoist heritage, a political system built on the rejection of liberalism as a political ideology, and here especially of the 'free' subject, of popular suffrage and private property ownership. Maoism emphasized the centrality of the socialist state in the making of political subjects, and it created a form of political citizenship rooted in rights to collective resources and realized in the appropriation of a script set out by vanguard elites to overcome personal and social limitations. This type of citizenship I call 'transcendental', as it is not suffrage that stands at its core, but the active emulation of political 'models', 'heroes' and even 'martyrs', in order to partake in the making of 'a new world'. Central to the formation of citizenship in rural China has also been Mao's administrative and political 'split' of the people into peasants (*nongmin*) and urbanites (*shimin*), with peasants forming the core of Mao's revolutionary mass subject. This Maoist heritage remains of central importance to understand contemporary strategies of citizen-becoming in what I call, following Frank Pieke, neosocialist China.[1]

In the following, I focus on the relation between, on the one hand, the reform state's ambitious aim to transform China from a country where 'politics [had been] in command' to a country 'governed by law' (*yi fa zhi guo*) and the emergence of a new 'citizen blueprint' (Keane, 2001) that propagates a newly individualized, self-regulating 'public person' (*gongmin*, i.e. citizen), and, on the other hand, the emergence of a self-propelled rural law activism that seeks to redress injustice and to hold local governments accountable to 'the people'. The protagonists of my paper are (next to the Chinese government) peasants who are ethnically Han as are the majority of all Chinese; in contrast to so-called national minorities (*shaoshu minzu*), they do not possess a nationally recognized culture that should be protected from China's modernization drive.

Nevertheless, China's peasants are today singled out as the owners of a collective 'custom-culture' (*fengsu*) that stands in tension with both the – particularly Chinese – culture-education' (*wenhua*) and the – universalist – civilization (*wenming*) of the desired new citizen (*gongmin*). Rejecting Maoist 'politics in command' meant that peasants are defined today mainly in terms of a 'problem' (*wenti*) of development and order, as a product of rejected political pasts lacking the essential quality (*suzhi*) for political subject-becoming: the link to the desired national future.

My paper is temporally located in the post-Maoist era of the 1990s and 2000s, where a government rhetoric of constructing 'development' (*fazhan*) and the 'rule of law' (*fazhi*) along with material, spiritual and political 'civilization' (*wenming*) faces a new peasant rights activism that appropriates legal knowledge to fight corruption, over-taxation, environmental destruction and, more and more, the expropriation of lands that, since the 1950s, have been owned by peasant collectives. James Holston (2008, p. 33) has argued that citizenship is a historical, situated process, involving assemblages of entrenched and insurgent forms, the latter unsettling the assumptions of the former, while inevitably being shaped and constrained by them. Much of the language and the symbolism used by activists is Maoist in nature, reflecting the fact that Mao made the peasants' liberation from bondage the precondition of China's liberation as a whole. But it is only from their localization as the collective cultural particular 'peasant' (*nongmin*) in the new society of 'citizens' (*gongmin*) that the insurgent nature of peasant law activism in neosocialist China can be understood.

Neosocialism brought forth a 'New Social' (Zhang & Ong, 2008) regulated increasingly through legal and market mechanisms, while, at the same time, it reaffirmed the Party's all-round definition power over the direction of the nation's 'development'. The result of this new type of governance in China was the rise of a new political discourse that focuses on problems of individual 'quality' (*suzhi*) and on collective cultural standards, rather than on correct ideology and the collective adoption of revolutionary social forms. This affected in particular the citizenship of peasants in China. Maoism administratively cemented the split between peasants and non-peasants (*feinongmin*), but elevated peasants to the revolution's collective mass subject. It claimed to have liberated peasants from bondage by giving them equal rights to newly collectivized lands and by making them participate in public (economic and political) work. Neosocialism, while allowing individual peasants freedom to move, to choose their economy and access to far wider information and promising them development and fair treatment under the rule of law, nevertheless denies them, as a category, political subjecthood because of their 'backward' custom-culture. Neosocialist China thus distinguishes between workers and peasant workers, entrepreneurs and peasant entrepreneurs, the former products of more advanced urban areas, the later of backward rural places (Xin, 2000).

In the following, I focus on citizenship struggles in rural China that increasingly tie themselves to the land question. Studies on the peasant condition in post-Maoist China have generally emphasized the peasants' internalization of the state's discourse of rural 'backwardness' as a kind of collective identity[2] (but see Kipnis, 1995). I shall argue, in contrast, that rural law activism constitutes a form of 'insurgent citizenship' (the term is Holston's [2008]) that emerged in response to transformations in neosocialist governance. Peasant activists and so-called 'peasant lawyers' (*nongmin lüshi*) use the language of law and legality to civilize local governments, to reverse their cultural exclusion and produce themselves as new peasant-citizens and thus as 'rightful' political subjects. Insurgent citizenship here means to appropriate the peasant label as a political position from where to formulate collective demands against the government, as well as to reinterpret central slogans of development from a local perspective. As I will show, legal activism mobilizes peasants as subjects for rights and creates a processual public sphere, involving journalists, academics, cadres and relevant others, where peasant campaigners can appropriate a 'collective voice'. The central government, not surprisingly, typically suppresses such activism precisely at that point under the pretence of upholding 'order'. Instead, it responds selectively to local grievances, presenting itself paternalistically as the protector of peasants and other 'feeble' groups and asserting itself as the sole owner of a solution to China's 'peasant problem' (*nongmin wenti*).

The ethnographic data on which this article is based were collected in an ongoing study ('The Social Life of Law, Peasant Lawyers and Formations of Justice in Rural China')[3] for which I led a large number of individual and group interviews with peasant lawyers and activists, travelled several weeks through their networks in Shandong, Hebei and Henan provinces and collected documentation of court cases, letters of complaints and newspaper articles they provided me with. I also draw on earlier research on local religion, urbanization and property rights in Fujian, southeast China.

'Collective incidents': territorial struggles as citizenship struggle in rural China

> Heaven and rich soil. Generation upon generation of ancestors, sons and sons of sons of the common people have been born out, grown on, and build their existence upon this soil. How many times, from the days of old until today, have the common people fought battles of resistance and shed blood over it! This red soil is soaked with fresh blood, in this black mud the bones of earlier generations have decayed.

With these lines the author of *Minyuan* ('People's rage') introduces his report of a legal battle, begun in 1994, against land expropriation in a Hebei village that follows the epic fight of two peasant 'heroes' (*yingxiong*) against an unresponsive, repressive and law-ignoring party bureaucracy. I met those two activists at their homes in 2006, when they had already become famous pioneers of legal activism to protect collective land rights, but had very obviously lost their own fight. All but a tiny amount of the village's original farm lands had been expropriated, the legal compensation money had not been paid and both lived in dire poverty in what had become a semi-urban, heavily polluted place. The report itself (Ren, 1999), like many similar to it, was repressed after its first publication, but circulated widely among the peasant law activists I met during my research in northern China. At that time, land expropriation had already become the main issue that propelled this activism itself, as it mobilized large numbers of affected villagers and evoked collective passions that drove peasants to join mass demonstrations, sit-ins, and more and more, in the words of lawyer Wang, to use the law as a 'weapon [*wuqi*] against those with power [*quan*] and money [*qian*]'. Wang was a 64-year-old 'peasant lawyer' (*nongmin lüshi*) whom I met in Shandong, and who had since the late 1990s helped fellow villagers to sue government cadres in over 700 court cases, reaching from legal suits against illegal taxation and fee taking, the abuse of power and violence, offences in relation to the one-child policy to, more and more, illegal land grabs and the embezzlement of compensation money. He told me that he had decided lately to limit himself to 'iconic' (*you daibiaoxing*) law suits that particularly mobilized rural people and represented the depth of China's peasants' problems. He was then working on a 'nine-village, 200-household' class action suit against illegal land grabs by a local government interested in road construction and another, 500-household class action suit concerning the embezzlement of compensation fees for the expropriation of farm lands.

In Western and Chinese imagination, 'earthbound China' has always been defined by the countryside and by agriculture. As productive resource and as ancestral territory, land has been the focal point of religious, kinship and community identities for 'generations upon generations', as the quote from *Minyuan* suggests, distinct from, and often in confrontation with, state-imposed histories and identities. Since the 1950s, the peasants' collective ownership of land has also stood for the state's recognition of peasants as political subjects with a particular claim on 'liberation'. Not surprisingly, the peasants' self-definition is closely linked to the land question, and public resistance to land expropriation has become an important moment to negotiate peasants' collective identity in neosocialist China. Chinese law does not recognize cultural difference; on the contrary, law has become an important tool to standardize social relations across the country and to emphasize the centrality of the state in the formation of social and political identities. Nevertheless, as Fong and Murphy argue, in the current political environment exclusion from cultural citizenship – from 'the right to belong to a broader community in ways that are felt by the individual and recognized by others' – can have 'devastating consequences', while at the same time a relaxation of social controls enabled marginal individuals to pursue social and cultural rights that transcend their legal, civil, and political citizenship (2006, p. 2). New struggles over China's land represent, as I will argue in the following, not a clash between peasant identities and modernity or between parochial interests and the general public as the dominant discourse in China suggests, but a struggle for renewed inclusion in the 'public' and for peasants' equal participation within the national project of 'development'. Insurgent peasant citizens fight against the loss of collective control over farmlands – which is not just an economic asset, but represent's Mao's fundamental gift of liberation to peasants – and, by using the law and legal means, they demonstrate, at the same time, ownership of relevant citizen knowledge. Land struggles have thus become a major arena where peasants seek to regain recognition as both peasants and citizens.

The land question and political mobilization

Despite the government's rhetoric of building 'political civilization' (*zhengzhi wenming*) and improving 'human rights' (*renquan*) by implementing 'governing through law' (*fazhi*) in China, confrontations between peasants and state power have escalated in number and scale, and in the 2000s so-called 'collective incidents' (*quntixing shijian*) became a daily occurrence in many parts of the country. A study conducted by the Chinese Academy of Social Sciences, quoted in the *China Left Review*, reports that between 2004 and 2005 land issues were the most common topic referred to in the Chinese media in relation to the 'three peasant problems' (*sannong*), and the study's selection of 130 'social disturbances' showed that 87 of them were rooted in land issues. For the first half of 2004 alone, government statistics show a number of 46,900 illegal 'land activities' (Zhao, 2008). This reflects a scale and speed of land expropriation that is likely to be without historical precedent. A BBC report from 2005 estimated that 'more than 66 million Chinese farmers have lost their land in the past ten years' (Griffiths, 2005). The report also briefly names the following incidents as representative of the ensuing social unrests:

- 6 November 2004: paramilitary troops put down an uprising of 100,000 farmers in Sichuan province.
- 10 April 2005: 20,000 peasants drive off more than 1000 riot police in Zhejiang province.
- 11 June 2005: six farmers die in a fight with armed men in Shengyou, Hebei province.
- 6 July 2005: several thousand farmers stand up to 600 policemen in Guangdong.
- 20 July 2005: hundreds of people near Beijing block the entrance to land assigned for use for the 2008 Olympics.

What triggers 'collective incidents' on such a massive scale? The Land Administration Law of the People's Republic, throughout its several revisions and amendments,[4] has persistently invested peasant collectives with the ownership of agricultural lands, and maintained that agricultural land can be transferred to non-agricultural uses only through a process of state requisition. As a result of a new market dependency by local governments, however, such regulations on land transfer have increasingly been circumvented. In highly industrialized regions like the Pearl River Delta, Guangdong, observers claim that 50 per cent of all industrial construction has taken place on formerly rural collective lands that never went through legal conversion procedures (Po, 2008, p. 1609). More importantly, as Peter Ho (2001) has argued, de-collectivization has blurred the understanding of which unit legally represents collective ownership in the new hierarchy of local administration: township, administrative village or villagers' group.[5] Triggered by what Ho calls 'deliberate institutional ambiguity', peasant collectives have undergone a process of 'silent expropriation' in terms of ownership rights, with *de facto* control over land being vested in higher levels of local government. The process of economic reforms thus involved both de-collectivization and centralization, of which only the former has been publicly acknowledged: the return to a market economy devolved land use and exchange rights to rural households who have been again made responsible for their own economy (a process also likened to rural 'democratization'), but *de facto* control over collective land became centralized in ever higher echelons of local government, which remain responsible for rural 'development' but are typically little responsive to villagers' concerns and life worlds.

Already under Mao, the expropriation of collectively owned lands was legal when it served 'public interest'; this remains the case today. But affected farmers often find their own interests (or that of 'peasants' in general) diametrically opposed to the politics of 'public interest' (*gong yi*) (Zhao, 2009) or 'development' (*fazhan*) in neosocialist China. In the vicinity of Xiamen City in Fujian province, where I did fieldwork in the 1990s and early 2000s, 'development' had meant that villages were cut in half by new six-lane highways or totally erased by the expanding city, farmlands destroyed and family homes razed for the construction of industrial zones, for golf courses and amusement parks, hills where family graves had been located were mined for the extraction of multicoloured granite and the sandy beaches villagers used for farming fish and shrimps dug up for building work in Xiamen City. Behind such expropriations stands often an alliance between private corporations and revenue-seeking local governments, which might habitually pocket large amounts of the legally mandated compensation fee.[6] Land issues today provide a major template for a grassroots political mobilization seeking to represent 'peasant interest'. In the CASS study, the expropriated peasant Li Zheng is quoted with the words that 'for a peasant family, land is not just in the interest of one generation, but of several generations. Therefore, all must help to defend it' (Zhao, 2008). In my research in Baisha village in Fujian Province, villagers who had lost their land in the early 1990s to a golf course, as well as also half of the promised compensation money, went several times to protest in front of Xiamen City's court of justice, women, men, children and old people, at the risk of being beaten and arrested by public security officers (as some were). In their collective petition they raised the age-old question the Maoist state had set out to solve – 'without land how can we and our children survive?'[7]

Scholars have noted that since the mid-1980s the slogans and tactics of peasant resistance have evolved from a 'weapons of the weak' tactic, to the strategic use of particular laws and appeals to solve particular problems, to more organized forms of resistance that use the law to achieve broader political ends (Yu, 2003). This seemed to have followed a trajectory of conflicts from the 'peasant burden' to land expropriation, and involved the formation of a new consciousness of peasants as a politically disenfranchised group no longer represented in government politics. Thomas Bernstein, quoting Hong Kong sources, shows that, during protests in Henan, Shanxi and Hunan provinces in 1995, radical slogans included 'all wealth of the land should go to the peasants', to 'end the exploitation and oppression of the peasant class' and 'long live the peasant communist party and the unity of the peasants'. A decade later, slogans called for the establishment of a 'peasant democratic government', a 'peasant land committee', a 'rural peasant land reform committee', a 'peasant revolutionary government' and even 'a TV station to give peasants a voice' (Bernstein, 2004, p. 13). At the same time, peasant protesters have evidently adopted means and manage relations far beyond the scope of both 'traditional' and Maoist peasants. As a study published in 2001 by the Central Committee's Organization Department states:

What is especially worthy of attention is that at present the frequency of collective incidents is rising more and more, their scope is broadening more and more, the feelings expressed are becoming fiercer and fiercer, and the harm they do is becoming greater and greater. . . . The organizational level is visibly becoming higher. Formerly, incidents were mostly spontaneous and fairly loose [*songsan*]. Now, many have leaders, are organized, and behind the participants there are core elements who exert influence and control. Some even hire lawyers and seek media support.

(Bernstein, 2004, p. 2)

The Guangdong conflict mentioned in the BBC report above is here of particular interest, as it demonstrates that an emergent alliance between peasants and urban human rights activists is forming around the issue of property dispossession in particular. Indeed, also the urban poor, who are evicted from their inner-city homes for the sake of 'development', today often rally in the defence of their citizen rights (Zhang, 2004), bridging the urban–rural split that divided 'the people' into two opposed sets of citizens. According to a report by the *Washington Post*, the Guangdong unrest started in the village of Taishi, once a farming community and now an industrial suburb of Guangzhou City, where farmers accused their government of embezzling the compensation money they had received for their expropriated lands, leaving them without either land or a retirement fund. At that point, the report continues:

> Yang and Lu, two veteran activists, quietly got involved in the struggle. They advised the Taishi villagers on what options where open to them under China's election laws.... Basing their demand on the election law and its recall provision, Feng and Liang [two local peasants] filed a formal recall motion on July 29.... Villagers gathered two days later in an open square. From atop a heap of bricks, as local reporters and other witnesses looked on, Feng read a section from the Chinese law books saying that village accounts must be published every six months and villagers had the right to recall [the village head]. 'The law will be our guardian,' he vowed.
>
> (Cody, 2005)

In the early twentieth century, Mao noted the readiness of many poor peasants to join the revolution. At the beginning of the twenty-first century, peasant activists employed Maoist language and Maoist symbolism, while at the same time turning to the law as 'weapon' and 'guardian', to resist their cultural and political expropriation as peasants and citizens and claim a fundamental right of equal participation in China's 'development'.

Struggles against the expropriation of cultural-political ('transcendental') citizenship

Traditional agriculture today carries little to no status in China. It hardly provides an income beyond the bare subsistence level, it is considered dirty work and work befitting the least qualified, or most 'backward' (*luohuo*), elements of the population. As a result, many of the 'peasants' engaged in land conflicts have long stopped working the land – such as the majority of Baisha's villagers, who had become rural entrepreneurs and whose main income source in the early 2000s was shrimp farming. Also the legal activists I encountered had often left agriculture at some point of their life in pursuit of a more meaningful task or a better life. Chen, a 38-year-old legal activist, always told me he wanted to be nothing else but a farmer. But he also related how as a younger man he had worked on construction sides in Qingdao and Weihai (two major cities in Shangdong), propelled there by dreams of personal development, of driving around in taxis, having a TV and eating good food. Instead, the working and living conditions were atrocious, and his boss never paid him. After two months he returned disillusioned to his village, where he later initiated a struggle against the corrupt and violent local party secretary. As he repeatedly rhetorically asked me in interviews: 'on what is China's development based? Who is building all these skyscrapers and modern apartments? Peasant workers [*nongmin gong*]. But still, peasants are denied citizen rights [*minquan*] and human rights [*renquan*] in China'.

Rural-urban migration in China is today often also a strategy to raise one's cultural and social citizenship, or 'quality' (*suzhi*), by exchanging life in a 'backward' rural place, defined by agriculture and peasantness, with a more 'developed', urban environment. However, such strategies are typically frustrated by urbanites who nevertheless classify 'peasant workers' as 'peasants', whose best contribution to national development is understood to be raw labour and whose efforts to adopt urban life styles are seen as fake and bound to failure (e.g. Yan, 2003). It is thus through migration that many rural people come to experience their 'collective peasantness' to be the source of a new exclusion from the political project of liberation – something perceived not just as 'unfair' (*bu gongping*), but, in the context of both the state's Maoist legacy and its recent 'legal turn' (*falühua*), as 'illegal' (*feifa*). While the discourse on cultural and political citizenship in neosocialist China suggests that at its core stands one's contribution to national development, the new discourse on law states that all citizens are fundamentally equal and should enjoy the same rights. Chen's statement above appeals to both these discourses, by arguing that, despite their contribution to 'development', peasants in China are today treated neither as equal citizens ('have no civil rights') nor even as *humans* ('have no human rights').

Why do land conflicts play such a role in expressing this sense of 'betrayal' and politically mobilizing peasants? As the quote from *Minyuan* suggests, rural land is the place where personal, familial, community and national memories intersect, where ancestors have settled and where they were buried, where ancestral halls and village temples were built as symbols of a place-based, collective identity and destiny. It is the place where rural people have experienced social membership as *bendiren* ('local-soil-people') and, since Mao, political subjecthood in a socialist collective with claims and obligations against its collective properties. For peasants, moreover, rights to collectively owned lands came to symbolize, under Mao, participation in the political project of 'liberation'. This was captured in the term *fanshen* (literally, 'to turn the body') that became popular during the period of the land reform. *Fanshen* implied most immediately a share in landed property and participation in collective production. But it promised much more that: a process of political subject-becoming. As Willian Hinton wrote in the epitaph to his eyewitness report on the revolution in a northern Chinese village:

To China's hundreds of millions of landless and land-poor peasants [*fanshen*] meant to stand up, to throw off the landlord yoke, to gain land, stock, implements and houses. But it meant much more than this. It meant to throw off superstition and to study science, to abolish world-blindness and learn to read, to ... establish equality between the sexes, to do away with appointed village magistrates. ... It meant to enter a new world.

(Hinton, 1966, p. xi)

In contrast, contemporary 'development', especially when it involves land expropriation, more often than not destroys the livelihood of the peasants concerned. It deprives rural collectives of land as their last valuable asset, it robs villagers of their reference for a common history and identity, and it symbolically strips peasants of the 'gift' of socialist citizenship. The manner of land expropriation suggests to many that their interest is no longer part of 'public interest', or, more emphatically, that the neosocialist state no longer considers them to be part of the 'public'. In the words of an elderly Fujian farmer, the government 'no [longer] cares about peasants' (*bu guan nongmin*). Those who protest against the expropriation of land therefore often invoke the spectre of total eradication of the peasant as a human, social and political subject.

Most of the activists I met, typically between 40 and 65 years old, had not spent all their life working the land, but, after experiencing a 'betrayal' (*pian*), they had emphatically embraced 'peasantness' as a political position. Engaging the law constituted for them not just a means to redress a particular injustice – a task for which the legal system was formally created, but in which it most often failed due to political pressure, especially when local governments were involved. Rather, engaging the law had the larger goal of addressing, and rendering public, the state's broken promise to bring 'development' (*fazhan*) to those with the largest claim on it – peasants. Among those who identified themselves with the 'peasant problem' (*nongmin wenti*) were demobilized soldiers, former and present village heads, teachers and formerly party secretaries, descendants of former landlords or of communists purged as legalists or capitalist-roaders in the 1950s, family members of arrested *falungong* members or former migrant workers who had experienced massive exploitation in the cities. Kevin O'Brien and Li Lijiang, who coined the term 'rightful resistance' to describe the new peasant legal activism, point to the impact grass-roots have on the formation of citizenship in China. But they argue that peasants should be 'thought of as occupying a position between subjects and citizens': because they do not consider 'rights to be inherent, natural or inalienable' and because citizenship demands are formulated as a 'claim to community membership [rather] than a claim to negative freedoms vis-à-vis the state' (2006, p. 122). Following Holston, I suggest instead that insurgent citizenship is always shaped by 'real-existing' historical formations of govern-ance and citizenship, rather than by the abstract liberal principles O'Brien and Li call on. In the case of post-Maoist China 'development' (*fazhan*) has become the universalist promise on which the legitimacy of the party state rests and the claim citizens hold against the government. But, extrapolating from the Maoist notion of liberation, *fazhan* relates economic, social, cultural and political transformation to the experience of personal and collective progress. While China succeeded in developing one of the fastest-growing market-driven economies, it transformed from a country with one of the world's smallest income gaps at the end of the Maoist era to one with the world's largest. This gap has, since the mid-1980s, become concomitant with an administrative 'split' between rural and urban areas, rural and urban household registers (*hukou*). Peasants, in this context, are depicted not just as poor, but as culturally 'underdeveloped' (*bu fada*).

Many of the legal activists I met in Shandong and Hebei provinces quoted illegal land seizures or the embezzling of compensation money as a proof of the absence of 'human rights' (*renquan*) or 'citizen rights' (*minquan*) for peasants in China. Because they fight for peasant rights at a high personal cost, they are often called 'heroes' (*yingxiong*), even by a sympathetic press, as they seem to represent a new type of rural leadership based on knowledge, sacrifice, self-esteem and loyalty to the peasant cause. Local governments, in contrast, typically view them as *diaomin* ('hard-as-nail-resisters'). Peasant activists share a common opposition to the political betrayal of China's peasants, as demonstrated in land grabs and the illegal acts of local governments. They also criticize legal advisers and judges working in rural China for 'caring only about making money', for having no political consciousness and for having a false perception of the law's purpose ('they don't understand the law'). As a group, however, these rural law activists are not simply anti-state or even anti-government. Rather, they are a diverse group of people, including those who actively reject the party state as a whole and hope for its immanent collapse, as well as (formerly) active members of the Communist Party or cadres in the local government, who see themselves as working at least on an idealistic level in the interest of the socialist state. Two further observations are important here. First, the activists' discourse on rights (*quanli*) and the 'rule of law' (*fazhi*) is almost inevitably linked with a concern for the building of a 'moderately affluent' (*xiaokang*) society, even with the creation of a new peasant (*xin nongmin*). All these are slogans and ideas promoted by the central government in China, which peasants are asked to embrace in their daily life. Second, rural law activists use the tools of law and the language of legality, in their own perception, in order to protect rural livelihoods, to discipline 'wayward' local government, to fight 'tyranny' (*canbao*), build a good society and to 'serve the people' (*wei renmin fuwu*). These are, of course, elements of a Maoist discourse that served to define the role of peasant's political activism during the Maoist era. Today peasants still build the 'new China' but are denied political visibility because of their lesser 'cultural citizenship'. Legal activism, in this context, seeks to reverse the peasants' cultural exclusion by re-radicalizing peasantness as a political position. Embracing peasantness and appropriating the language of law and legality are central to such a 'reversal'.

Cultural scripts and legal activism: a new politics of 'liberation'

Citizenship in China, as elsewhere, is a historical process shaped by a particular assemblage of the modern, as well as a field of cultural construction and political struggle (Holston, 2008). The specific articulation between politics and culture that shaped governance and political subjecthood in modern China was that of 'liberation' – of the nation, of the people and, more recently, of the entrepreneurial individual. Politics and law were defined as liberatory not because, as in liberal thought, they were seen as reflecting the deeper humanity of free individuals, but because they were a gift that a political vanguard gave to the Chinese people to transform themselves so that they could realize a 'new', strong and sovereign China. 'Under the Nationalist Party-state [1912–49]', as Jerome Bourgon has argued, 'law remained basically a device for "correcting the mores and practices" at the hand of a civilizing centre, rather than an attempt to reshape rights blooming in the social and economic life. . . . [R]ights were evoked with the intent to strengthen the state and make the nation more compact' (2004, p. 112). With the advent of socialism in China, a new politics of 'liberation' sought to transform a politically debilitated 'national population' (*guomin*) into 'the people' (*renmin*) – the ideal socialist, politically sovereign collective. Mao, known for his anti-legalism,[8] saw in radical politics and class struggle the means to liberate the Chinese from the Four Olds (*si jiu*: old culture, old customs, old habits and old thinking) so that they could become the *fons et origo* of communism in China. Deng Xiaoping's push in the early 1980s for 'legalization' (*falühua*) aimed initially, rather pragmatically, at regulating the emerging market economy and at rebuilding political stability after the Cultural Revolution. But, as the range of new legislation expanded, law, together with the market itself, became the preferred – if formally de-politicized – tool for creating a new citizen (*xin gongmin*) better suited to the 'socialist market economy with Chinese characteristics' than the 'outmoded', collectivized socialist masses (Keane, 2001). The new national goal was now 'development' (*fazhan*), defined, along the lines of 'liberation', as an economic, political and cultural process rooted in the active appropriation of 'advanced' (*xianjing*) knowledge and practices by its citizens. 'Democratic centralism' (*minzhu jizhongzhi*) continues to assert that only a vanguard centre can make decisions in the interest of 'the people' (*renmin*), that the primary task of a politics of liberation is the elimination of 'backwardness' in society and that only those who fully embrace this politics can hope to experience 'citizenship' as participation in the sovereign power of the state.

The politics of liberation in the twentieth century brought forth 'the peasant' as a central subject of politics. When radical republican elites in the late nineteenth century adopted science (*kexue*), politics (*zhengzhi*) and law (*falü*) as tools for state strengthening and nation-making, a primary task became to define the backward cultural aspects at the root of China's problem of nation-becoming. As Myron Cohen writes, it was then that the peasant (*nongmin*) was 'invented' as:

> a major obstacle to national development and salvation. For [communist and non-communist elites alike], rural China was still a 'feudal' society of 'peasants' who were intellectually and culturally crippled by 'superstition'. Through the transformation of 'farmers' into 'peasants', 'tradition' into 'feudalism,' and 'customs' or 'religion' into 'superstition' there was invented not only the 'old

society' that had to be supplanted, but also the basic negative criteria designating a new status group, one held by definition to be incapable of creative and autonomous participation in China's reconstruction.

(Cohen, 2005, 62–3)

According to John Flower, in the following decades '[r]ural backwardness and the peasant question became not just a pragmatic problem to be solved, but also the symbolic realm through which competing visions of China's cultural identity were defined' (2002, p. 46).

In contrast to the first republic, the communist revolution took root in the countryside, and declared the peasantry as 'the popular base of the revolution'. The creation of the household register system (*hukou*) in 1956 froze all unauthorized movement between city and countryside, and created different forms of socialist citizenship for peasants and non-peasants (*feinongmin*). While urbanites worked in state-owned factories or the state bureaucracy with rights to a state pension, the peasants' life world was defined by their particular collective, where they maintained claims and obligations of political and economic participation. As Dorothy Solinger writes:

by the early sixties, people were definitively pinned into position, as the walls around the city thickened and hardened; 'peasant' and 'urbanite' became unbridgeable classifications. Regardless of the actual content of their labor, only those in cities could be called 'workers'; all those in the rural areas, whatever their occupation, were stamped 'peasants'.

(Solinger, 1999, p. 222)

Political struggle, however, cut across the categories of Maoist 'split citizenship'. Peasants were now thought of as having a 'dual nature':

on the one hand, as an exploited class of labourers, the peasants were a powerful revolutionary force in the struggle to overthrow capitalism, imperialism and the feudal system of exploitation, on the other hand, as smallholding producers the peasants were subject to all the narrow conservatism, short-sighted egalitarianism and acquisitive capitalism of the petty bourgeoisie, and as such, were a suspect class.

(Flower, 2002, p. 47)

Maoism's political legacy has been, nevertheless, that it made the peasant as a political subject thinkable, placed the 'peasant problem' at the centre of a politics of liberation and thereby linked the political liberation of the peasantry tightly to the liberation of Chinese society itself.

The government today propagates a 'new peasant' (*xin nongmin*) as the solution to the problem of underdevelopment of the countryside. In an article published by China's main government organ, 'self-reliance' and 'independence' from the state (*zhubenxing, dulixing*) are named as the main differences between the new and the traditional peasant, personal traits which, in a strikingly (neo)liberal mode, are defined as 'natural human characteristics'. Through party leadership and state education, in conjunction with the 'competitive pressure' and the 'profit motive' of the new market economy, new peasants are to develop 'innovative spirit', 'entrepreneurial conscious-nesses, 'initiative', 'openness' and 'comparative judgement', following workers and urban areas (Chen, 2005). At the same time, slogans such as 'send law down to the countryside' (*song fa xia xiang*) – with *song* also meaning 'gift giving' – have constructed law as a gift of modernization from the state to those in need of it. In 1986 the first of a number of five-year programmes to popularize the law (the so-called *pufa* campaigns) was inaugurated. But, as the 1985 'Resolution on the Basic Dissemination of the Knowledge of Law' demonstrates, *pufa* campaigns have sought to create a self-regulating, civilized citizen rather a rightful one, a subject amenable to national economic development:

> the core element of socialist modernization is the build-up of the economy; there is an urgent need for persons who know and understand the laws, who ... have also learned how to apply legal remedies in order to guarantee the smooth progress of the economic [system's] reform. The dissemination of statutory knowledge emphasizes precisely these objective requirements.
>
> (quoted in Exner, 1995, p. 78)

Deng's reforms allowed 'bodies' to circulate more freely in space, breaking down the geographical boundaries between urban and rural places. They made peasants in the early 1980s the first to enter market relations and to experience a weak form of private ownership in the form of land contracts, while urbanites continued to live and work in the state sector and their urban *danwei* ('unit'). But peasant activists interpreted the marketization and de-collectivization of the rural economy, especially when compared with urban areas, retrospectively as a proof of the state's increasing indifference to rural development and peasant welfare. Even the introduction of 'grassroots democracy' in rural areas first and foremost aimed at peasants' *liberalization* – their 'cutting off' from the state – rather than their *liberation*. The 'Organic Law on Village Committees', passed in draft form in 1987 and as official law in 1998, allowed every peasant over the age of 18 years to elect a new committee of village representatives. Significantly, it was first introduced in poorer areas with few industrial developments, serving political stability by involving villagers in the selection of local representatives, while placing blame for poor economic performance onto their own incapacity and 'bad' choices. Political authority has remained with the village party secretary, who is typically instituted by the township government (Oi, 2004, pp. 276–8). Peasant and citizen are in colloquial speech often simply opposed, with a peasant being identified as someone who 'does not understand' (*bu dong*) and 'has no culture-education' (*mei you wenhua*). I also frequently heard villagers make similar statements, as an explanation for their own disempower-ment. This was no simple self-stereotyping, but reflected the fact that to the present day only peasants with a college degree are allowed to apply for formal urban employment, and thus to become citizens (in the double sense of the term). 'Liberalization', in a context of transcendental citizenship, thus did not result in the fuller citizenship of rural people but threatened to sever peasants' link to the project of citizen-becoming. As a result of culturally fixing them in lesser civilizational space, and diverting responsibility for their collective 'liberation-development' away from the state, peasants are increasingly addressed as mere subjects for labour (see Yan, 2003).

Reversals

What were the techniques that law activists employed to reverse this kind of exclusion and present themselves, again, as subjects for politics and bearers of 'liberation'? As the government discourse did, peasant law activists focused on law and economy as origins of both a 'new world' and 'new peasants'. But rather than seeing new peasants as emerging from their engagement with the market, activists generally condemned Deng Xiaoping's rural reforms as politically disabling, as the reason for peasants' new difficulty 'to get together' and for the invisibility of their contributions to national development. In contrast, law has increasingly become the political arena where the boundaries and shape of a 'new world' are being defined. Chen, the 38-year-old activist, described as his goal also the creation of a 'new peasant'. He thought his own 'quality was too low' (*suzhi tai di*), as he had left middle school without a degree, but he hoped, with the help of retired teachers, local NGOs and his network of journalists and lawyers, to create a village school where peasants could learn about new farming techniques and more general skills, but also receive legal education and, hopefully, become 'active' themselves. The school was part of his larger plan to recreate a cooperative that would allow peasants to 'get together' (*heqilai*) to defend their own economic and political interests. His cooperative had already a large library of mostly legal texts and a number of active members from different villages, including a blind man who was known as an activist for the rights of handicapped people.

In their belief that ordinary peasants lack knowledge, independence and agency, rural activists reiterate the official discourse on the peasant problem and the opposition between traditional and (yet to be constructed) 'new peasants'. Lawyer Wang often complained that his fellow villagers did not 'believe in the law' (*bu xiangxin falü*). He opposed beliefs in 'superstition' with a belief in the law, which in his view was also different from political 'propaganda'. Another lawyer, who stressed that he was 'not superstitious in the law' (*bu mixin falü*), suggested that law was like a sword to be wielded against those with money and power. But the difficulties and hardship legal activists encountered in suing local governments demonstrated to all that, still, 'money and power were bigger than the law' (*qian bi fa da*; *quan bi fa da*) in China. The government's strategy of propagating 'governing through law' has certainly here found a local form, and provided many of the slogans (for example, to 'use law as a weapon' or the call for a 'new peasant') taken up by legal activists. But rather than being examples of 'rule consciousness' (Perry, 2007),[9] such appropriations allow rural law activists to present themselves as 'bearers of the universal' and to enter into a dialogue with the state, while formulating a particular claim on 'liberation'. A crucial difference, moreover, lies in how rural law activists interpret peasants' lack of 'development': not as a failure of culture, but as a failure of politics, and a result of state neglect. Returning to the village meant for many of them to embrace peasantness as a particular political position, from which to launch a new movement for peasants' recognition within the national project of development. Not surprisingly, many of their meetings ended with the singing of old revolutionary songs, where the word 'people' (*renmin*) had been replaced by 'peasants' (*nongmin*). Peasant lawyers, often more reserved and individualistic than activists, have become pivots in re-capturing political 'peasantness' from below. Their legal knowledge supports a whole network of activists, and their victories, especially in cases involving the violation of peasant rights, inspire more and more people to 'believe in the law' (*xiangxin falü*), and become its 'missionaries'.

How shall we understand in this context the re-appropriation of Maoist slogans and symbols, post-Mao? Not as Mao nostalgia, as I shall argue, but as part of the effort to reposition oneself as both peasant and citizen, that is, to reclaim political subjecthood for the peasant category in contemporary China. Whereas the government regards law as a tool to shape personal morality and culture, I was often struck how peasant law activists saw in law mainly a means for political transformation. Maoist policies were often described to me as Maoist law, and the passing of hundreds of new laws after the reforms interpreted not so much as civilizatory progress but as a reflection of the multiplication of problems after the economic reforms, rooted in a political situation where cadres no longer 'serve the people'. A former village head, whom I met working together with 'peasant lawyer' Wang, for example, showed me the over eighty paragraphs of strong new Land Administration Law to convince me of the number, depth and complexity of land conflicts in contemporary China. Lawyer Wang himself used a business card that introduced him as a 'People's Republic of China Peasant', and that had Maoist slogans such as 'to serve the people' and 'men and women are equal' printed on the back. Several reports had appeared on him in the local press, in law reviews and even on national TV, after which he was virtually flooded with requests to take on cases. Jokingly, he often complained how strenuous it was to 'serve the people', that he was tired of it and that it should be the government's job. Many activists also saw part of their work as being to memorize relevant laws paragraph by paragraph, either individually or in local study groups reminiscent of the groups studying Mao's little red book. One particularly experienced 'veteran', whom I met in his Hebei village, had visited on his bike departments of justice at different levels of the government more than fifty times to submit petition letters, including in Beijing, where he had spent a total of two months at the famous – now destroyed – 'complainants village' (*shangfang cun*) that housed thousands of peasant activists from all over China. Having gained notoriety with local cadres, he was now running a 'science and technology' (*keji*) farmers' association in his village, whose members regularly studied legal documents he had obtained through various means. They were at that time studying the police law, which, as I was assured, was particularly hard to get hold of. He told me that they wanted to memorize it so that they could quote paragraphs from it 'in the face' of a public security officer they might find violating the law.

It is precisely Maoism's history of transforming the peasantry from a cultural other into a political force of liberation that grants Maoist symbolism an important role in rural legal activism. Many of the legal activists I met displayed posters and busts of Mao in their homes, and all those I met actively lived 'simplicity' (*pusu*) – again a Maoist political term that highlighted the socialist ideal of simple living and frugality embodied by the Chinese peasantry. None of them, for example, smoked, many did not drink or drank only moderately (something highly unusual for rural men) and all claimed to prefer simple food to the delicacies served in restaurants. As one activist put it, non-indulgence was his way to 'struggle' (*dou*) against the 'big eating, big drinking' (*dachi, dahe*) attitude of cadres and the *nouveaux riches* that is commonly associated with the squandering of public resources. Another one, who proudly displayed a Mao poster at his door, told his party secretary directly that under Mao he 'would have already been dealt with'. For experienced law activists, who emphatically reject being *shunmin* (obedient subjects), the stakes of engaging the law have long been political. Such stakes can involve, beyond a victory in court, regaining one's dignity by standing up to cadres, and demonstrating one's citizenship by understanding the rule of law (*fazhi*) and resisting local 'bullies' (*ba*). They might see themselves as doing the work of the government by fighting against corruption and for the preservation of the public good. But they also produce themselves – and their clients – as knowledgeable 'new citizens', and thus recreate a subject that neo-socialism rendered impossible: a peasant and a citizen. Finally, rural power relations are being rebalanced as legal activism brings forth new types of local leaders whose knowledge of 'rights' and strategic experience, and whose sheer persistence in taking on local governments, is opening a 'protective umbrella' sought by many of their fellow villagers.

Beyond 'split citizenship': appropriating a voice in an activists' public sphere

In his book *Politics and the other scene*, Étienne Balibar (2002) approaches the problem of political action through 'three concepts of politics' – emancipation, transformation and civility – and their complex interaction.

Whereas emancipation and transformation might be called the 'proper' place of politics, civility becomes a politics when it creates public and private spaces for the politics of emancipation and transformation. The rural law activists I met not only sought to engage law as a vehicle of the political in contemporary China; engaging the law also profoundly expanded the social, political and geographical agency of all rural activists and, despite consciously appropriating the 'label', all had expanded their social, political and geographical agency far beyond the enclosures that so long defined 'peasantness' in China. Lawyer Wang, for example, continued to live with his wife in a two-room, simple village home that belonged to his brother, who worked in the nearby township. On Sundays he would still tend to his cornfields, although most of the agricultural work was now undertaken by his wife, his two sons and their wives. He wore typical peasant attire, including simple cotton shoes, and during the cold winter months spent much of the time sitting on the *kang*, a traditional northern Chinese heated bed, the only heating in his house. But he owned two mobile phones that he used for legal counselling and for keeping in contact with different government offices, academics, activists and journalists, that contained more than 400 contacts and that were always switched on. He spent most of his days travelling to courts and clients in different parts of the province, although he used the cheapest forms of transportation and accommodation. Moreover, he owned a full-blown electronic office set up in his bedroom at home, including a computer, a copy machine, printer, scanner and fax, and permanent broadband access. He stored written documents, reports, films and photos relating to his legal work on the computer, used email to be in contact and give legal advice to peasants from other parts of the province and even the country, and searched the internet for legal documents or policy statements pertinent to his cases. Already in his sixties, Wang had learned how to use a computer from a younger neighbour, but the equipment itself had been donated by a German foundation, with the help of a German professor of law, who had read a report about Wang in the law journal *Fazhi ribao* (Legal daily). Wang frequently searched the net for reports about himself. Since he defended his first case in the mid-1990s, more than twenty Chinese newspapers had reported about him, law students frequently visited him and even the main national TV station had broadcast a special report on him. He had a pile of name cards from roughly 100 journalists, lawyers and other academics on his desks. I met him because he stayed in close contact with a professor from the Chinese University of Politics and Law. Some years ago, the country government had also made him into an official 'law propaganda worker', although, as he told me with a grin, it was mainly in order for them to 'save face'.

Chen, the much younger activist, who often relied on the legal advice of Wang and other peasant lawyers, instead made a point of dressing 'smart' so that people outside his village would not immediately recognize him (and dismiss him) as a peasant. He was a regular at conferences on the 'three agrarian problems' (*san nong*) organized by academics and NGO activists, and saw himself as a general activist for peasant rights, education and welfare. While maintaining that he was 'only a peasant' and 'wanted to be nothing else', he maintained important contacts with journalists at local and regional newspapers, who supported and regularly reported about him; one of them had even acted as his witness in court. Journalists had reported on his court cases – he had sued cadres for corruption, abuse and violation of the environmental and land law, and was himself being sued for stirring up 'local unrest' – and written about his attempts to organize and collect funds for his various peasant welfare initiatives. What turned him into a 'peasant hero' (*nongmin yingxiong*), and made him infamous with his local government, was his stubbornness in returning to 'the law' and suing local cadres at whatever cost, even after having spent a total of nine months in prison, his livestock and crops destroyed, his family threatened and most of his savings lost on his court cases.[10] 'I am not afraid', he often said to me, 'I am not doing anything illegal'. Like Wang he was using the internet for information and for collecting articles about himself as well as for browsing the local press to find names of other peasant activists. His shrewd use of legal knowledge, scare tactics and wide support network had eventually turned him into a 'leader' others would seek out for strategic advice or support. He had also turned into an important intermediary between the village world and wider world of 'peasant politics' in China, which he often brought into his village in the form of student delegations, sympathetic lawyers, teachers and academics.

Both Wang and Chen are examples of peasant activists who have managed to reach beyond the confines of 'split citizenship' in China and, as part of their own political transformation, to represent the 'peasant voice' in a still heavily restricted, but incipient activists' public sphere in China. This public sphere depends on the emergence of a new investigative journalism on the sub-national level, often driven by public outrage over 'corruption', the burgeoning rights discourse and the readership's interest in stories depicting local villains and 'heroes'. Wang and Chen have become part of this public sphere because they speak the shared language of citizenship, national interest and prestige – the language of progress, law and legality – and thus can represent a kind of insurgent 'new peasant'. But, this voice, as well as the public sphere they are part of, is sustained only in and through the activism itself. Being stigmatized as peasants and thus as culturally backward, there is no permanent 'slot' reserved for the peasant voice in contemporary China. Should they be forced, or choose, to become 'inactive' the 'larger' public sphere they were part of simply collapses – as happened to lawyer Wang after he suffered a stroke – public attention shifts elsewhere and the village again becomes the main horizon of agency. Peasant activism has been successful in forcing the Chinese state to grant more political attention to the situation and 'burden' of Chinese peasants in the process of economic reforms, but neosocialist 'split citizenship' continues to exclude peasants as a cultural collective from 'developed China', and thus denies them political subjecthood. As my paper has tried to show, such an exclusion can be reversed only by positioning oneself within a particular community, defined by a common experience of political marginalization, while reaching beyond its limits to engage with the particular national discourse of citizen-becoming.

Notes

1   For some time now Chinese scholars have debated the question whether China is becoming neoliberal or not. Those who argue against the idea of a neoliberalism 'with Chinese characteristics' have pointed to the lasting power of the party state, its ability to define national futures and its interventions in society, and to the absence of an entrepreneurial class independent of the party in China (Kipnis, 2007; Nonini, 2008). In choosing the term neosocialist, I follow Frank Pieke to argue that the type of governmentality taking form in China has 'roots in both socialism and neoliberalism' (2009, p. 126).
2   I thank one of the reviewers of this article for pointing this out to me.
3   I thank the Nuffield Foundation, UK, for a Small Research Grant, and Oslo University for its 'start pakke' grant that made this research possible.
4   For an English translation of the current Law Administration Law, see, for example, the webpage China.org.cn (http://www.china.org.cn/english/environment/34345. htm).
5   Township, administrative village and villagers' group (or 'natural village') are the organizations that have, after the introduction of the Household Responsibility System for rural land lease in the 1980s, replaced the former communes, brigades and production teams. In the period of people's communes, it was the production team (the predecessor of today's 'villagers' group') which acted as owner. The dismantling of collective enterprise and the return to a 'private' economy especially at the lowest level made this legal title no longer self-evident (Ho, 2001, pp. 400–1).
6   Jing Jun, who studied enforced relocation in relation to the building of the Great Dam, reports that planners had already figured in 'anticipated consequences' (2007, p. 150) like the embezzlement of funds when they calculated the overall government expenditure for relocation.
7   From a collective petition by Baisha villagers, Fujian, 1998.
8   Mao's early attempts at socialist legality were soon abolished for movement politics, so that arbitration committees stressed the mass line rather than referring to particular laws or regulation (see Lubman, 1999, ch. 3).
9   I owe being alerted to Perry's argument to a lecture given by Li Lijiang at the University of Lund in November 2009.
10   While Chen was not deterred by these 'costs', many peasants are forced to give up, or even deterred from becoming activsts in the first place, considering the costs such activism carries for their families, especially their children. One told me that such activism is therefore typically something for older people, who have already paid for their children's education and wedding arrangements.

References

Balibar, E. (2002). *Politics and the other scene*. London: Verso.
Bernstein, T. P. (2004). Unrest in rural China: A 2003 assessment (pp. 1–21).
Center for the Study of Democracy, University of California at Irvine.
Bourgon, J. (2004). Rights, freedoms and customs in the making of Chinese civil

law, 1900–1936. In W. C. Kirby (Ed.), *Realms of freedom in modern China.* Stanford, CA: Stanford University Press.

Chen, Y. (2005). Xincheng nongmin: xin nongcun jianshe de zhuben liliang. Retrieved 20 September 2009 from http://news.xinhuanet.com/politics/2005-12/14/content_3918043.htm.

Cody, E. (2005). Chinese hold protest leader, land activist. *The Washington Post.*

Cohen, M. L. (2005). *Kinship, contract, community, and state: Anthropological perspectives on China.* Stanford, CA: Stanford University Press.

Exner, M. (1995). The convergence of ideology and the law: The functions of the legal education campaign in building a Chinese legal system. *Issues and Studies, 31*(8), 68–102.

Flower, J. (2002). Peasant consciousness. In P. Leonard & D. Kaneff (Eds.), *Post-socialist peasant? Rural and urban constructions of identity in Eastern Europe, East Asia and the former Soviet Union.* New York: Palgrave.

Fong, V. L. & Murphy, R. (Eds.) (2006). *Chinese citizenship: Views from the margin.* London and New York: Routledge.

Griffiths, D. (2005). China faces growing land disputes. Retrieved 15 January 2009 from http://news.bbc.co.uk/2/hi/asia-pacific/4728025.stm.

Hinton, W. (1966). *Fanshen: A documentary of revolution in a Chinese village.* Harmondsworth: Penguin.

Ho, P. (2001). Who owns China's land? Policies, property rights and deliberate institutional ambiguity. *China Quarterly,* (166), 394–421.

Holston, J. (2008). *Insurgent citizenship: Disjunctions of democracy and modernity in Brazil.* Princeton, NJ: Princeton University Press.

Jing, J. (2007). State comrades and an elderly woman's suicide. *Critique of Anthropology, 27*(2), 146–63.

Keane, M. (2001). Redefining Chinese citizenship. *Economy and Society, 30*(1), 1–17.

Kipnis, A. B. (1995). Within and against peasantness: Backwardness and filiality in rural China. *Comparatives Studies in Society and History, 37*(1), 110–35.

Kipnis, A. B. (2007). Neoliberalism reified: Suzhi discourse and tropes of neoliberalism in the People's Republic of China. *Journal of the Royal Anthropological Institute, 13*(2), 383–400.

Lubman, S. B. (1999). *Bird in a cage: Legal reform in China after Mao.* Stanford, CA: Stanford University Press.

Nonini, D. M. (2008). Is China becoming neoliberal? *Critique of Anthropology, 28*(2), 145–76.

O'Brien, K. J. & Li, L. (2006). *Rightful resistance in rural China.* Cambridge: Cambridge University Press.

Oi, J. C. (2004). Realms of freedom in post-Mao China. In W. C. Kirby (Ed.), *Realms of freedom in modern China* (pp. 264–84). Stanford, CA: Stanford University Press.

Perry, E. J. (2007). Studying Chinese politics: Farewell to revolution? *China Journal, 57.*

Pieke, F. N. (2009). The production of rulers: Communist party schools and the transition to neo-socialism in contemporary China. *Social Anthropology, 17,* 125–39.

Po, L. (2008). Redefining rural collectives in China: Land conversion and the emergence of rural shareholding co-operatives. *Urban Studies, 45*(8), 1603–23.

Ren, Y. (1999). *Minyuan.* Beijing: Zhongguo Wenlian Chuban Gongsi.

Solinger, D. J. (1999). China's floating population. In R. MacFarquhar & M. Goldman (Eds.), *The paradox of China's post-Mao reforms* (pp. 220–40). Cambridge, MA: Harvard University Press.

Xin, L. (2000). *In one's own shadow: An ethnographic account of the condition of post-modern reform rural China.* Berkeley: University of California Press.

Yan, H. (2003). Neoliberal governmentality and neohumanism: Organizing suzhi/value flow through labor recruitment networks. *Cultural Anthropology, 18*(4), 493–523.

Yu, J. (2003). Dangdai zhongguo nongmin de weiquan huodong yu zhengzhi. Unpublished paper.

Zhang, L. (2004). Forced from home: Property rights, civic activism, and the politics of relocation in China. *Urban Anthropology and Studies of Cultural*

Systems and World Economic Development, *33*(2–4), 145.

Zhang, L. & Ong, A. (Eds.) (2008). *Privatizing China: Socialism from afar.* Ithaca, NY: Cornell University Press.

Zhao, B. (2009). Land expropriation, protest, and impunity in rural China. *Focaal, 9*(54), 97–105.

Zhao, L. (2008). Significant shift in focus of peasants' rights activism. *China Left Review.* Retrieved 16 January 2009 from http://chinaleftreview.org/index. php?id=7.

Subjectification and education for quality in China

Andrew B. Kipnis

Abstract

Education reform is perhaps the arena of discourse in which Foucauldian themes of subjectification are most explicit. Questions of what type of adult (citizen/subject) the education system should produce are directly articulated. From the point of view of social analysis, however, the actual production of subjectivities in schools remains a relatively opaque matter. Not only do many contradictory strands of political discourse exist side by side, but, even more importantly, the impact of these discourses on actual pedagogic practice is not direct. Moreover, it is doubtful that any pedagogic practice has the subjectifying effects that educators imagine. This paper examines educational rhetoric and practice in China's 'education for quality' (*suzhi jiaoyu*) reforms. It finds a contradictory mix of subjectifying rhetoric and practice in China's classrooms and suggests that discerning the types of subjects that are being produced in China's classrooms is far from an easy task.

Taking up initiatives articulated in Foucault's writings (Foucault, 1979, 1983, 1988, 1991), Paul Rabinow (1984) uses the word 'subjectification' to emphasize the interrelation among scientific modes of classifying people, the dividing practices of governments, and the means by which human beings objectify and act upon themselves, that is, see and create themselves as particular types of human subjects. Also taking inspiration from Foucault's writings, writers interested in neoliberal governmentality have described processes of governing that are imagined to work through individuated subjectivities by engaging the capacities for self-discipline of individual subjects (e.g. Hoffman, 2006; Rose,

1996; Shore & Wright, 2000). Comparing these two closely connected but slightly divergent bodies of literature raises questions about the relationship between neoliberal imaginings and the processes of subjectification that take place among people governed in regimes that articulate neoliberal ideals, that is, about the relationship between the preferences for entrepreneurial, responsible, self-governing subjects expressed in the speeches of political luminaries or policy documents and the actual production of such subjectivities. Sometimes the existence of political discourses for creating neoliberal subjectivities alone is taken as evidence that such subjects are actually produced, as is the case with John Gledhill's claim that neoliberal cultures of audit have led to a 'deep neo-liberalization' of the world in which the 'whole of social existence and personhood' is 'desocialized' (Gledhill, 2004, pp. 340–341), a view I have criticized elsewhere (Kipnis, 2007, 2008). Such writings gloss over processes of subjectification by ignoring both actual practices of policy implementation and, more importantly, the practices of social exchange that take place within the context of social relations where the policy is implemented. Other scholars convincingly demonstrate that neoliberal discourse can be taken up by the people to whom practices of neoliberal governmentality are applied, as is the case in Lisa Hoffman's examination of the subjectivities of young job-seekers in China (Hoffman, 2006, 2008).

In this article, I examine a case where neoliberal ideas expressed by policy entrepreneurs (and to some extent circulating in society at large) are not actualized among the people to whom the discourse is applied. More specifically, I focus on the subjectification of schoolchildren who are subject to the educational rhetoric and practice of China's 'education for quality' (*suzhi jiaoyu*) reforms. The education for quality reforms are part of a larger field of governing known as *suzhi* discourse (Judd, 2002; Kipnis, 2001, 2006, 2007; Murphy, 2004; Woronov, 2003; Yan, 2003). Over the past two decades, the concept of *suzhi*, usually glossed as 'quality', has become increasingly central to dynamics of culture and governance in the People's Republic of China (PRC). Reference to *suzhi* justifies social and political hierarchies of all sorts, with those of 'high' quality being seen as deserving more income, power, and status than those of 'low' quality. The term may be applied to individuals or groups of people, and is often used to refer to the entire population of a given nation or region. The birth control policy speaks in terms of raising the quality of the Chinese population by limiting its quantity. In rural contexts, cadres justify their right to rule in terms of having a higher quality than the 'peasants' around them (Thøgersen, 2003). All manner of human resources decisions can be justified in terms of quality, and development projects may be bolstered by claims that they will raise the quality of the targeted poor (Yan, 2003). In popular usage, the notion of 'lacking quality' is used to mock or discriminate against those as various as rural migrants, litterbugs, short people, the nearsighted, and the poorly-dressed. Individual Chinese of many backgrounds consume a dizzying variety of books, nutritional supplements, clothes, exercise equipment, medicine, and educational programs in the pursuit of quality for themselves and their children. Overall, the Chinese Communist Party (CCP) increasingly claims its own legitimacy in terms of its ability to produce a strong and powerful nation by individually and collectively raising the quality of its citizens. During the late 1980s, education reformers bought into this discourse by coining the term 'education for quality' (*suzhi jiaoyu*) and in 1999 succeeded in having education reform at all levels legally mandated under this slogan (Kipnis, 2001, 2006).

The education for quality policy and the discourse surrounding it have been quite stable, in part because the term 'quality' is extremely vague and a wide variety of specific policies can be justified in education for quality rhetoric, and, in part because some of the basic structural contradictions of the Chinese education system, especially the factors that encourage the fevered pursuit of exam success, have persisted (Kipnis, 2011). The 1980s arguments that led to the policy have resurfaced throughout the 1990s and 2000s. In addition, many of the specific policy actions associated with these arguments have reappeared in different schools and localities again and again, in a cyclical, 'campaign' style.[1]

Focusing on education reform is theoretically useful because it is an arena of discourse in which Foucauldian themes of subjectification are quite explicit. Questions of what type of adult (citizen/subject) the education system should produce are directly articulated. From the point of view of social analysis, however, the actual production of subjectivities in schools remains a relatively opaque matter. Many contradictory strands of political discourse exist side by side and the impact of these discourses on actual pedagogic practice is not direct. Moreover, it is doubtful that any pedagogic practice has the subjectifying effects that educators imagine. Moving beyond the types of subjects that are idealized in political rhetoric to actual processes of subjectification requires careful analysis.

Foucauldian analysts of neoliberal discourse define it not as the rejection of all forms of governing but as a form of governing that attempts to 'responsibilitize' subject/citizens, to remake the people it governs into autonomous subjects who will be entrepreneurial, democratic, and law-abiding, and take responsibility for their own health and welfare (Dean, 1999; Foucault, 1991; Gordon, 1987, 1991; Hindess, 1996a, 1996b; Rose, 1996). While such discourse no doubt has a place in China, its opposite, authoritarian discourse, also thrives. Rather than subjects that will produce themselves as responsible, autonomous actors, authoritarian discourse desires subjects that will obey the whims and dictates of a sovereign, in this case the CCP. The sovereign alone evaluates the desired goals of governing, as the autonomy of the people to decide what is responsible is not to be trusted (Sigley, 1996, 2004; Tomba, 2008). Gary Sigley (2006) has described how neoliberal forms of govern-mentality can coexist with authoritarian forms of government in China (and elsewhere). Here, I argue that the coexistence of neoliberal and authoritarian discourses leads to neither a coherent model of governing nor a single form of subject. Rather, the various techniques of governing lie in irresolvable contradiction with one another. The agents that implement education policy struggle with contradiction more than resolve it.

The next section of this paper examines different aspects of education for quality policy in relation to what in the above terms could qualify as neoliberal and authoritarian discourses of governing. The third section moves on to processes of subjectification that occur in Chinese schools and highlights the importance of the production of social relations to processes of subjectification.

Methodologically, to link governing discourses to subjectifying process, I rely upon both the analysis of academic debates about educational practice and the ethnographic observation of educational practice. I have conducted research in Zouping, a rapidly industrializing rural county in Shandong province, since 1988 and spent time in Zouping schools in 1999, 2000, 2005, 2006, 2007 and 2009.

Governing discourse and educational practice

One of the primary themes in the literature on 'education for quality' is the case for replacing a memorization-based education system with one that teaches creativity and reasoning (Cui, 1999; Kipnis, 2001). During the late 1990s, Chinese TV shows on education bemoaned the inability of the Chinese education system to produce creative entrepreneurs like Bill Gates. One Shandong parent I interviewed reproduced an argument I had heard on such a TV show:

> Bill Gates didn't even go to university. When he was young he spent all of his free time experimenting with computers. He didn't have to spend all of his time memorizing useless information in the preparation for university entrance exams. In China, even primary-school children are forced to memorize many things. How can China possibly produce a Bill Gates?

In reaction to such arguments, during the late 1990s many school districts began holding special 'creativity' classes as part of the regular school curriculum for primary-age students. Scores of articles in education journals suggested activities for such classes, such as posing questions with no definitive answer, and then encouraging the children to come up with as many different answers as they could think of. Other articles simply advocated more free time for children, so that they could think up their own playtime activities. Often, authors of newspaper and academic articles drew contrasts with western countries, where children were said to never have to memorize anything and to have many more hours of playtime (Liu, Zhang & Fang, 1997). These arguments further led to a nationwide campaign to reduce the homework burden (*jianfu*) of Chinese students (Woronov, 2003). At least at a rhetorical level, this call to educate students to be more creative and entrepreneurial appears to be a fairly straightforward instance of neoliberal governmentality.

The popular Chinese belief that such education practices originate in the West and require China to learn from western nations likewise fits with governmentality theorists' arguments that see neoliberalism as a discourse originating in western forms of government (see, for example, Dean, 1999, pp. 209–210).[2]

The seeming overlap between *suzhi* discourse and neoliberal governmentality is reinforced but also complicated when one looks at the works of Chinese authors who relate *suzhi* to political liberalism instead of just economic entrepreneurship. Jie Sizhong (2004), for example, argues that a '*suzhi* crisis' of the Chinese nation is preventing the political maturation of China and the emergence of a liberal political system. To allow liberalism to emerge, Jie suggests that the *suzhi* of the Chinese people must be raised by cultivating the following qualities: an independent personality, a strong sense of self-consciousness, a liberation of individuating characteristics, self actualization, self-respect, a spirit of tolerance, a spirit of freedom, the spirit of equality, the spirit of democracy, the spirit of law, human rights consciousness, and a consciousness of citizenship. Jie urges the government to adopt policies that will develop these qualities, especially in the realm of 'education for quality' (Jie, 2004, pp. 139–180). Though arguably different in terms of social ideals, the political liberalism of Jie and neoliberalism that emphasizes entrepreneurship and financial self-discipline converge in their desire to cultivate individuals that exercise psychological autonomy and a willingness to take responsibility for their own decisions. In terms of their implications for teaching in school, both suggest comparable modes of cultivating autonomy that could be described in terms of neoliberal governmentality.

If these instances of *suzhi* discourse may be labeled as neoliberal governmentality, then the authoritarian aspects of *suzhi* discourse can be seen as existing in those practices, attitudes, and proclivities that this discourse targets for reform. Here the work of Børge Bakken (2000) illuminates. He argues that through its implementation of enforced regimes of imitation and rote memorization, socialist governing in both the Maoist and post-Mao eras has produced close associations between notions of education, order and discipline. He theorizes the role of 'exemplary models' in Chinese education and governing and demonstrates the importance of emulating models in the processes whereby the government labels certain villages, cadres, and families as models, in the manner in which handwriting and calligraphy students are taught to copy written characters, in the way in which teachers are called upon to put themselves forward as models (*wei ren shibiao*), in the way in which the exam-oriented education system emphasizes memorization, and in many other aspects of life. In contrast to neoliberal desires for citizen subjects that will think independently, be tolerant of difference and entrepreneurial, in the processes of governing that Bakken describes, the purpose of education appears to be to produce a citizenry that will follow the models the government puts forth unthinkingly. LeVine and White (1986) take this argument further by suggesting that authoritarian education practices are typical of agrarian societies, and that the evolution away from such systems of education commonly occurs in processes of industrialization. In LeVine and White's argument, too, we can see parallels to the Foucauldian finding that neoliberal governmentality is a cornerstone of modernity.

Such an evolutionary argument, however, does not really fit the situation in contemporary China. While an opposition between an education system designed to produce a liberal, entrepreneurial citizen-subject and one designed to produced an authoritarian subject is useful to understanding polemics about education reform in contemporary China, it is too simplistic to associate *suzhi* discourse only with neoliberalism or to announce that China is slowly but steadily making the transition away from authoritarianism to liberalism in its education system. First of all, though the advocates of a less memorization-based education system are numerous, it does not appear that they have been at all successful in implementing such reforms after more than a decade of trying. Obstacles to implementing such reforms exist both in higher levels of government and in the everyday tactics of the governed population. As one popular saying has it: 'Education for quality is flashy, but exam-oriented education is solid' (*Suzhi jiaoyu honghong lielie, Yingshi jiaoyu zhazha shishi*). Secondly, (and in contradiction to this saying) there are ways of using the notions of *suzhi* to argue for a more memorization-based education system or even a more authoritarian education system. As another popular saying goes: 'Education for quality is an empty frame, anything can be stuck inside it' (*Suzhi jiaoyu shi yi ge kuang, shenme dou wang limian fang*).

The problems of assuming a neoliberal content to the education for quality reforms are especially apparent in the field of political education. There, authoritarian and liberal goals coexist in contradictory tension with one another. For example, along with entrepreneurialism, one of the ubiquitous types of qualities that *suzhi* education policies are to cultivate is a high level of 'ideological *suzhi*' (*zhengzhi sixiang suzhi*). Depending on who is describing ideological *suzhi*, this category can be considered to be constituted by items as diverse as loyalty to the CCP, love of country, respect for the law, the ability to resist bourgeois liberalization, a democratic spirit, a Marxist worldview, an atheistic worldview, and so on. Some of these items are similar to those on Jie's list of the qualities needed for producing a modern, liberal, democratic citizenry. But others are clearly not. For example, when writing on the topic of inculcating loyalty to the Party, some advocates of education for quality emphasize that we must make students recognize the need to maintain communist Party leadership. One method for accomplishing this goal is to teach a version of history in which the only possible conclusion is that without the actions of the CCP there would be no new China (Cui, 1999, p. 118). A second is to promote love for the nation, love for the Party, and love for socialism through a primary school curriculum that emphasizes the evils of imperialism, the accomplishments of socialism, the beautiful places in China, and the symbols of the nation and the Party (Cui, 1999, p. 134–135).

The contradictory mix of liberalism and authoritarianism in the education for quality literature exists not just in the content of what is to be taught, but also in the manner in which the content is to be taught. On the one hand, as suggested above, much of this literature emphasizes open-ended discussions, child-centered classrooms, and other non-authoritarian classroom practices. However, those who write about teaching political education deflect these suggestions with reminders that with regard to political attitudes teachers must keep 'one hand hard, and another hand soft' (Cui, 1999, pp. 116–117). Such authors warn that when discussing issues like whether a Marxist materialist worldview is superior to a religious worldview (one that includes beliefs in gods or spirits), the teacher must ensure that all classroom discussion ends with a pure affirmation of the former (Cui, 1999, p. 133).

An explicit contradiction between the 'authoritarian' and 'liberal' aspects of education for quality became apparent to me when I was touring schools in Shandong in 2000. Most of the schools had their hallway walls covered with black-and-white portraits of Marx, Engels, Lenin, Stalin, Mao Zedong, Deng Xiaoping, Jiang Zemin, as well as various famous scientists and Chinese patriots. As an Australian parent used to seeing bright school hallways filled with colorful student artwork, these schools seemed incredibly dreary. But I understood the portraits as an instantiation of Bakken's theory of the use of exemplary models – children are to be exposed to larger-than-life heroes. Everyday student artwork is too flawed to be displayed in the same space as the images of such perfect beings. The display of such portraits is also explicitly advocated in the literature on inculcating high ideological *suzhi* (Cui, 1999, pp. 139–140).

One experimental junior high school I visited, however, did have the walls covered with student artwork, essays, and projects (Kipnis, 2001). Not a single portrait of a socialist leader or famous scientist was to be seen. The principal of this school explained to me that she was following the *suzhi*-raising education principles of encouraging student initiative, taking a student-oriented approach to education, and demonstrating to the students that their efforts and initiatives mattered in shaping the world. In one of the few cases of teaching independent organizational skills in China that I have ever heard of, this principal also had her students plan and run their own athletic meets, school plays and social clubs. When I described the hallway decorations of the experimental junior high school to the principal of another school, he wondered how students could learn the proper respect for the Party and develop a high degree of ideological *suzhi* in such an environment. He argued that by displaying the portraits of socialist leaders and scientists on the walls, students learn who they should respect.[3]

That these opposing viewpoints were expressed only when I forced the contradiction into the open demonstrates the sensitivity of the issue. There are very few explicit debates in the 'education for quality' literature, especially in regards to political education. When discussing this topic, some authors will include contradictory examples right after one another, suggesting that 'faith' (*xinren*) in the Party and independent thinking are easily integrated 'qualities' (*suzhi*) that can and should be taught at the same time (e.g. Guan, 2003). Others demonstrate their liberal thinking not by explicitly declaring their objections to teaching 'faith' in the Party, but by refusing to mention this 'faith' in their lists of qualities that should be taught. The Shandong Province research group on education for quality, for example, uses the category of 'thought and morality *suzhi*' (*sixiang daode suzhi*) rather than ideological *suzhi*, and makes no mention of either faith in the Party or love for socialism as qualities to be inculcated (Shandong Yanjiu Ketizu, 1998). Finally, some others demonstrate their authoritarianism by emphasizing faith in the Party and love for socialism as the most important qualities to be taught (e.g. Ma, 2001; Xiong & He, 2002). But no one explicitly writes that faith in the Party or socialism and independent thinking are contradictory. To do so would be to exceed the limits of what is permissible to express in public in contemporary China.

That no one dares to express this contradiction, however, should not fool us into thinking that Chinese governing is a single non-contradictory blend of authoritarian and liberal techniques.[4] Rather, as implied by the different decorative choices of the two principals, as well as the different emphases of various authors on the topic of political education, sometimes the application of one technique excludes the application of another, and a choice must be made. That individual teachers can be painfully aware of this contradiction was made clear to me by a senior middle-school political education teacher whose class I had attended in 2005.

The lesson I witnessed was part of the mandatory curriculum and had been taught as long as the teacher could remember. It involves an analysis of the 'contradictions' involved in the transformation of an egg into a chicken.[5] The lesson is famous enough to have become a source of humour for irreverent satirists like Wang Shuo (see Wang, 2000, p. 228). It compares the role of the internal factors (a fertilized chicken egg), with external factors (a conducive environment, particularly in terms of the appropriate temperature). While conceding that both factors must be present for the transformation to occur, the lesson concludes that the internal factors are the basis for the transformation and, thus, more important. Both the teacher and the textbook finally apply these terms to other contemporary and historical political problems, such as the internal contradictions and external environment of economic development in China. Though the teacher spoke eloquently and did his best to apply the 'education for quality' principles of involving the students in discussion rather than simply lecturing, none of the students appeared to have grasped the logic of the discussion. No one could come up with a correct answer to any of the teacher's questions and getting the students to volunteer any sort of answer was like pulling teeth. I, too, had difficulty grasping why the internal and external 'factors' (*neiyin* and *waiyin*) should be called 'contradictions' (*maodun*), and why, even if one concedes that the internal factor is more important in the case of the chicken and the egg, that it should always be the case that the internal contradiction is most basic.

After the class the teacher sighed and told me that teaching thought and politics is always difficult. The content is abstract and serious (*yansu*), he said, and it is always difficult to spur on classroom discussion. I commiserated with him and shared the difficulties I encountered when teaching unmotivated undergraduate students. I then asked why he did not use the education for quality technique of encouraging the students to discuss the lesson in a more free-form style. Could he not just put them into small groups and let them decide what was a contradiction and how the internal and external factors related to one another?

He replied by acknowledging that such an approach would perhaps work in other classes, but quickly added that it was really out of the question for a thought and politics class. He pointed out that this particular lesson came from some of Mao Zedong's most important essays.[6] But, I asked, had not the Party already admitted that Mao had made errors in the past? He replied that this was the case, but that these errors were not taught to middle-school students. More importantly, the Party line on this aspect of Mao Zedong Thought was clear: the lesson was both absolutely correct and a treasure of the Chinese people.[7] Besides, on the standardized exam there would be only one possible correct answer on this topic and it would do the students no good to pretend otherwise.

The next time we met, the teacher deepened his analysis. He told me that the students' intellectual *suzhi* could be raised much more quickly if it were possible to approach thought and politics as items for real, open debate. Unfortunately, he said, this approach would not improve their ideological *suzhi*. So, he joked, the Chinese student could be thought of as a hatching chicken produced by the internal contradiction between intellectual and political *suzhi* and the external contradiction produced by too many students wanting to attend university and the resultant competition in the University Entrance Exams.

This example shows how authoritarian and neoliberal teaching techniques are not simply blended into a single smooth system of governing, but exist in mutual contradiction with one another in a context where some people might attempt to choose or champion one of them over another. This is true despite the facts that Chinese educators label all of these techniques with the singular title 'education for quality', that the Chinese state declares its education system to be entirely 'socialist', and that some academics describe the Chinese education system as thoroughly 'neoliberal' (e.g. Anagnost, 2004).

In another school, I discovered an education for quality class that complicates the relationships among socialism, authoritarianism, neoliberalism and education for quality even further. This class blended what Bakken or LeVine and White might see as authoritarian teaching techniques with a viewpoint that much of the official curriculum was too authoritarian. The principal of this school had explained to me how the school was implementing an education for quality program by moving away from a memorization and test-based curriculum and towards a curriculum where creativity was emphasized. While this was to be done in all classes, she explained, the creative aspects of the curriculum were to be reinforced in special twice-a-week creativity (*chuangxin*) classes. She then invited me to sit in on a fourth-grade creativity class. In this class, the teacher first read from a book of Tang dynasty poems. The students then chanted the poems in unison after the teacher. Next individual students were invited to stand up and repeat the poems aloud for the entire class. The teacher corrected the students' pronunciation of standard Mandarin and gave suggestions about how to read with more emotion. Over the course of a 40-minute class, three poems were recited in this manner. Absolutely no time was spent in discussing the meaning of the poems, though the teacher did write a few of the less common characters on the chalkboard and briefly discussed their meanings and usage.

After the class I asked the teacher whether the students ever wrote their own poems, either in class or for homework. She explained that, as this was a creativity class, there was no homework. But, I objected, given that this was a creativity class, shouldn't the students be creating something of their own instead of just memorizing Tang dynasty poems? She replied that she thought of the class as a 'quality-raising' (*suzhi*) one, and added that the parents felt that nothing raised the students' quality like Tang poems. Later, when I asked one of the students' mothers why the students were memorizing poems in a class that was supposed to be devoted to creativity, she chided me for taking the word 'creativity' too literally. First of all, she said, students enjoy Tang poems much more than some of the other things they have to memorize, so this class satisfied the education for quality principle of making education enjoyable. Second, even if students did not understand the poems now, they would appreciate them after they grew up. It was later in life that the poems would make the students more creative. Finally, she argued that in contrast to the politically-oriented, official history the students had to memorize in other parts of the curriculum, Tang dynasty poems were truly something that would improve the students' quality.

This parent thus made explicit the logic behind the whole scheme. For her, it was not the fact of a memorization-oriented curriculum that made the education system seem authoritarian and socialist, but the matter of *what* was being memorized. When the students had to memorize the CCP's official version of history, then the education system seemed authoritarian to her. Thus, this woman could be described as not accepting the distinction between neoliberal and authoritarian education methods that inform much of the discourse about the education for quality reforms. But she still considers the education system to be too authoritarian and wishes to reform it in a direction that she would consider to be less authoritarian.

These debates over the interpretation of the meaning of 'education for quality' and even actual classroom practices associated with the educational reforms remain a step removed from social relations and practices of subjectification. But they demonstrate the multivocality both within *suzhi* discourse and the routes by which this discourse is translated into classroom practice. By no means can the education for quality campaign be conceived as a simple matter of 'socialism' ending and 'neoliberalism' beginning. To definitively trace the route from classroom practice to actual processes of subjectification is perhaps an impossible task, and certainly would require a long-term, longitudinal study of subject-making among students. But based on ethnographic observations, I will suggest some of the pathways this route might take.

From teaching to subjectification

In large part, at least during the period of my research, the 'education for quality' reforms were not successful in reducing the importance of exams, memorization and homework in the education system, especially at the secondary level. The reforms did result in reductions in the level of homework at the primary-school level in some places, and changes in some of the content of the curriculum. But even if educational practice remains 'authoritarian' in many ways, it is not at all clear to me that authoritarian classroom practice leads to the production of authoritarian subjects. While I saw many forms of subjectivity emerging from Zouping's schools, none struck me as government-obeying robots.[8] Three forms of subjectivity stood out as being particularly significant.

Perhaps most important of these were filial subjects. At Zouping's secondary schools in the mid-2000s, students studied from 12–15 hours a day, seven days a week. Their routines were extremely regimented, with all studying taking place in mandatory study halls. Most students lived in dorms at their schools and were in scheduled activities from 6.00 am until 10.00 pm, seven days a week. In my conversations with hundreds of students, I met none who said that they enjoyed this routine. But most pushed themselves to the limits of their endurance to succeed. If asked why, one common reply was that they did it for their parents, who desperately wanted them to go to university. Household surveys that I undertook in the region confirmed that parental desire for children to attend university was universal.[9] Teachers, whose performance evaluations in part depend upon the exam performances of their students, reinforced this morality by telling students that they should think of their parents whenever they were tempted to ignore their studies. Even the curriculum had a role in promoting this moral vision, with explicit lessons devoted to filial piety in both 'thought and morality' (sixiangpinde) and literature classes. One of the Tang dynasty poems all Shandong sixth-grade students memorize, for example, is titled Youzi Yin.[10] It describes an old mother sewing clothes for her son by candlelight so that he can spend all of his time studying and become an official in a faraway place. Students are taught to memorize the poem so that they can read it aloud with feeling, to imagine the sacrifices that their own parents make on behalf of their education, and to write essays about how they might repay their own debt to their parents.

Charles Stafford (1995) describes how textbook examples of filial piety in Taiwan during the late 1990s likewise emphasized parents sacrificing so that their children may study. As in *Youzi Yin*, the predominately gendered pattern of these examples involved "textbook mothers" sacrificing for their sons' academic success (Stafford, 1995, p. 70). But Stafford suggests that in Taiwan, such examples implied sacrifice by the family for the nation. In contemporary Zouping, parents, teachers and students alike understand this sacrifice as a matter of familial self-interest rather than as a sacrifice by the family for the nation. In Zouping, educational success is above all a familial success, and the production of disciplined students is understood by parents, teachers and students alike as the crafting of filial subjects.

To a certain extent, the drive to reach university has rendered many of the debates over education for quality moot. From the point of view of gaining admittance to university, secondary education is a competitive game. Educational reformers can tinker with the content of the curriculum and the method of its delivery all they like, but the primary purpose of the game from the vantage of the participants will not have changed. This drive to reach university is also perhaps the primary factor behind the inability of schools to reduce homework amounts. With admittance to university being based on examination, societal pressures to compete in these exams have rendered reductions in homework difficult to implement.[11] In short, in this instance it seems that societal-based processes of subjectification influence practices of educational delivery more than the other way around.

But sometimes classroom practice can appear to have subjectifying effects, as would seem to be the case with the emergence of homeroom identities, the second type of subject that stood out for me. One of the earliest arguments against exam-oriented education by education for quality advocates was that it made teachers ignore below-average students. These researchers argued that since less than 15 per cent of students had a realistic hope of entering university, when teachers are evaluated on the basis of how many of their students test into university, then teachers ignore the bottom 50–60 per cent of their students.[12] Consequently, the students who need the most attention from teachers are likely to receive the least amount of it (see, for example Liu et al., 1997). To correct this tendency, as one common slogan has it, education for quality requires teachers to 'face the entirety of the student population' (*mian xiang quanti xuesheng*), instead of just devoting attention to the outstanding students (Yu, 2003, p. 240).

The methods recommended for reaching out to all of the students are numerous, but one of the most popular ones is to treat the class as a collectivity. One way of treating the class as a collectivity involves reinforcing rather than eliminating traditional educational practices. As one junior middle-school maths teacher explained to me, an emphasis on drill and repetition is often boring for the best students, who can master a given mathematical skill relatively quickly. But making everyone in the class work through hundreds of similar problems ensures that quite a few of the mediocre students will be able to keep up with the best students. Thus, at least for some teachers, the education for quality principle of emphasizing creativity and that of facing the entirety of the student population can seem contradictory.

Collective classroom identities are reinforced by the entire structure of educational delivery in Zouping. Homeroom classes of students stay together for the entire year. Schools are quite large and contain between two and ten homerooms full of students at every grade level. A homeroom full of students stays put in their own classroom for most of the school day while teachers of various subjects move in and out from one period to the next. Homerooms compete with one another in terms of test scores in all classes, athletic events, and all manner of extra-curricular activities. If you ask a Zouping student what year of school he or she is in, the response will include both the year and the homeroom, as in 'junior middle school year two class five' (*chuer wuban*). The term 'same-class schoolmate' (*tongban tongxue*) is used to depict the relationship among classmates in single homeroom, and implies a high level of camaraderie. When I asked one junior middle-school student why same-class schoolmates were more important to her than her other classmates, she said: 'school in China is so hard and boring. It is just work, work, work all day long. When you suffer like that together with people in the same room, when we help each other get through the hard days, it just makes you closer'. In brief, the egalitarian aspects of exam-oriented education, including repetitive drill and mandatory, collective study halls, subjectifies students as members of particular homerooms with classmates who are particularly likely to be their friends.

For the third type of subject production, consider the subjectifying effects of the utter failure of the education system – school drop-outs. In Zouping, the intense exam-oriented pressure of the education system leads to 5–10 per cent of students dropping out of school before completing the nine years of compulsory schooling. Quite often this occurs in year 8 (the second year of junior middle school). I interviewed a number of school drop-outs during my time in Zouping, and all of them emphasized the exam pressure (rather than the economic factors that are more important in impoverished areas) as the reason for dropping out. One 18-year-old young woman, now a hairdresser in the county seat, explained: 'School just isn't for everyone. All the teachers care about are your test scores, and if you don't test well you aren't important. All day long it is just study, study, study; can you imagine living in a boarding school like that when you aren't a good student?' A 20-year-old man, working as a waiter at a restaurant, told me:

> My parents really wanted me to go to university, but I just couldn't do well at school. I couldn't understand what the teachers were saying and I didn't like to study. In year seven there was one test after another. If I wasn't the worst-scoring student in the class I would be the second or third worst. I couldn't see the point of simply memorizing books, that's not what life is about. Who wants to be a bookworm [literally book-idiot, *shudaizi*]? I told my parents that studying

was just a waste of time for me as my grades would never improve; they weren't happy, but what could they do? Maybe some day I will go to vocational school and become a chef. I've heard that they will let you in now even without a junior middle-school graduation certificate.

These statements reproduce some of the criticisms of exam-oriented education described above. But more importantly, especially in the case of the young waiter, they point to another common subject position in contemporary China, that of the practical person (usually man) of action, conceived of partially in opposition to and partially as a complement to the 'intellectual' or 'book idiot'. Such people are depicted in countless novels, television shows and movies and have deep historical roots in China's long traditions of oral and written narratives. Their characteristics usually involve an emotional and verbal directness that is manifested by speaking whatever they think at a given moment. They are frequently depicted as impatient, willing to act quickly on partial information, loyal (though sometimes shrewd), street-smart, and embedded in local networks with many other such operators. They often criticize intellectuals for their hesitancy in action, their indirection in expressing their feelings or opinions, and their lack of practical, forms of 'how to' knowledge – especially those that involve embeddedness in local social relations, knowing who to contact to get something done. Ironically, it is these subjects who come closest to the entrepreneurial neoliberal ideal, despite the fact they leave school. Thus another, perhaps necessary, result of exam-oriented education is the production of people who fail exams and who find it relatively easy to subjectify themselves as people of action, embedding themselves in local networks of social relations with other such people, especially if they are male. For women who fail at school, the position of caregiver, whether as housewife, auntie, hairdresser, nursemaid, or sex worker, may likewise seem an alternative social position to the book idiot.

Conclusions

This paper has examined a variety of cases of subjectification in relation to governing discourses in the education for quality reforms. These discourses include a variety of contradictory elements that have translated unevenly into actual practice over the past decade. But regardless of the particular frame in which the policies are justified, or even the extent of a given policy's success or failure, the on-the-ground processes of subjectification always involve the give and take of social exchange and long-standing narratives of social roles and relations not mentioned by the policy itself. Thus, while policy undoubtedly influences the ebb and flow of social relations, it never translates into subjectivity in an unmediated fashion.

The role of social relations in processes of subjectification is especially problematic for discussions of neoliberal governmentality. Truly autonomous, self-reliant subjects do not exist. Whatever policies are justified in the name of neoliberalism and however they are implemented, they will always result in some form of social relations and these social relations will always generate subjectivities that are relational, interactive and social. Thus, as Comaroff and Comaroff (2000) suggest, the results of neoliberal policy will always be ironic and counter-intuitive. For anthropologists it is perhaps no surprise that processes of subjectification occur through social relations and in the context of stereotyping, long-standing narratives about how those social relations play out. But for the theorists who link policy discourse with processes of subjectification, this is an often-ignored dimension. That education policy is an arena in which explicit theories of subject formation are often articulated does not enable any shortcuts to the understanding actual processes of subjectification.

Social theorists interested in neoliberal governmentality are certainly justified, however, in arguing that policy discourses circulate across many levels of society. In the case of education policy, these discourses are picked up by education administrators, teachers, parents and even the students themselves. As Hoffman shows (2006, 2008), job-searching students are just as able to create narratives of entrepreneurship and self-reliance about themselves as neoliberal politicians. The gaps and contradictions in this *suzhi* discourse, however, allow plenty of room for manoeuvre. Governing agents at many levels of society can link concerns with raising the quality of the people to those with entrepreneurialism, creativity, ability to work well in groups, loyalty to country or the Party, traditional gender roles, or almost anything else. In the PRC, where authoritarian government leads to outward mimicry of the terms of official policy, the ability of a single form of governing discourse to become multivalent is even more extreme (Kipnis, 2006, 2007). The fact that governing discourses are a melange of contradictory elements, rather than a single regime of truth, both facilitates the circulation of governmentalities and limits the power of scholars who examine texts about governing but not social relations to illuminate processes of subjectification.

Notes

1 See Bennett (1977) for the classic description of policy campaigns in China.
2 For a critique of this view see Kipnis (2008).
3 By 2005, when I revisited the same schools, the 'liberal' principal had retired and a compromise had been enacted throughout the county school district. All schools had spaces devoted to scientists and Marxist heroes as well as space devoted to model student artwork. None encouraged or even allowed students to plan and run their own social activities.
4 Ong and Zhang (2008) insightfully note how self-fashioning and authoritarian governing coexist. This coexistence, however, should not be taken as a coherent, planned system of governing.

5   A written text for this lesson can be found in the thought and politics textbook for the first semester of the second year of senior middle school (Xiaoxue Sixiang Pinde He Zhongxue Sixiang Zhengzhi Jiaocai Bianxie Weiyuanhui, 2003, pp. 118–126).

6   In particular see Mao's essay 'On contradiction' (Mao, 1975, vol. 1, p. 341).

7   Note that Mao Zedong Thought is not a matter of what Mao thought or wrote, but rather the official interpretation of Mao's writings by the contemporary Party propaganda apparatus. There is, of course, much room for reading Mao's writings on education in an anti-authoritarian, even anarchist manner.

8   See works by Nie (2008) and Rosen (1989, 1994) for more on how official political education fails. However, to say that obedient robots are not produced is not to say that patriotism is not enhanced. This patriotism is not necessarily pro–Party and can come out in ways that both support and undermine Party rule.

9   For more on my research methods see Chapter 1 of Kipnis (2001).

10   The poem and accompanying didactic material may be found in the year-six first-semester literature textbook (*Yuwen*, Book 11, Shandong: Renmin Jiaoyu Chubanshe, 2005, pp. 77–81).

11   Other authors who write about the exam pressures Chinese students face include Liu et al. (1997), Woronov (2003), and Naftali (2009). Many documentary films now depict the pressures in Chinese high schools including *Senior Year* (*Gao San*) directed by Zhou Hao, distributed by the University Services Centre at the Chinese University of Hong Kong.

12   The 15 per cent figure comes from the 1990s. Now almost 25 per cent of a given age cohort in Shandong can attend university and perhaps 50 per cent have a 'realistic chance' of attending. See Bai (2006) for a discussion of the expansion of university places in China.

References

Anagnost, A. (2004). The corporeal politics of quality (suzhi). *Public Culture*, *16*(2), 189–208.

Bai, L. (2006). Graduate unemployment: Dilemmas and challenges in China's move to mass higher education. *The China Quarterly*, (185), 128–44.

Bakken, B. (2000). *The exemplary society: Human improvement, social control, and the dangers of modernity in China*. New York: Oxford University Press.

Bennett, G. (1977). China's mass campaigns and social control. In A. Auerbacher, S. Greenblatt & R. Wilson (Eds.), *Deviance and social control in Chinese society*. New York: Praeger.

Comaroff, J. & Comaroff, J. L. (2000). Millennial capitalism: First thoughts on a second coming. *Public Culture*, *12*(2), 291–343.

Cui, X. (Ed.) (1999). *Suzhi jiaoyu: Zhong xiao xue jiaoyu gaige de xuanlu*. Jinan: Shandong Jiaoyu Chubanshe.

Dean, M. (1999). *Governmentality: Power and rule in modern society*. London: Sage.

Foucault, M. (1979). *Discipline and punish: The birth of the prison*. New York: Vintage.

Foucault, M. (1983). The subject and power. In H. L. Dreyfus & P. Rabinow (Eds.), *Michel Foucault: Beyond structuralism and hermeneutics* (2nd ed., pp. 208–226). Chicago: University of Chicago Press.

Foucault, M. (1988). *The history of sexuality* (R. Hurley, Trans). New York: Vintage.

Foucault, M. (1991). Governmentality. In G. Burchell, C. Gordon & P. Miller (Eds.), *The Foucault effect: Studies in governmentality* (pp. 87–104). London: Harvester Wheatsheaf.

Gledhill, J. (2004). Neoliberalism. In T. Nugent & J. Vincent (Eds.), *A companion to the anthropology of politics* (pp. 332–348). Malden, MA: Blackwell.

Gordon, C. (1987). The soul of the citizen: Max Weber and Michel Foucault on rationality and government. In S. Lash & S. Whimster (Eds.), *Max Weber: Rationality and modernity* (pp. 293–316). London: Allen & Unwin.

Gordon, C. (1991). Governmental rationality: An introduction. In G. Burchell, C. Gordon & P. Miller (Eds.), *The Foucault effect: Studies in governmentality* (pp. 1–52). London: Harvester Wheatsheaf.

Guan, Z. (2003). Tan xiandai nongmin suzhi jiaoyu. *Xinyang Nongye Gaodeng Zhuanke Xuebao*, *13*(1), 77–8.

Hindess, B. (1996a). *Discourses of power: From Hobbes to Foucault*. Cambridge, MA: Blackwell.

Hindess, B. (1996b). Liberalism, socialism and democracy: Variations on a governmental theme. In A. Barry, T. Osbourne & N. Rose (Eds.), *Foucault and political reason: Liberalism, neo-liberalism, and rationalities of government* (pp. 65–80). Chicago, IL: University of Chicago Press.

Hoffman, L. M. (2006). Autonomous choices and patriotic professionalism: On governmentality in late-socialist China. *Economy and Society*, *35*(4), 550–70.

Hoffman, L. M. (2008). Post-Mao professionalism: Self-enterprise and patriotism. In L. Zhang & A. Ong (Eds.), *Privatizing China: Socialism from afar* (pp. 168–181). Ithaca, NY: Cornell University Press.

Jie, S. (2004). *Zhongguo guomin suzhi weiji*. Beijing: Zhongguo Changan Chubanshe.

Judd, E. R. (2002). *The Chinese women's movement between state and market*. Stanford, CA: Stanford University Press.

Kipnis, A. (2001). The disturbing educational discipline of 'peasants'. *The China Journal*, (46), 1–24.

Kipnis, A. (2006). Suzhi: A keyword approach. *The China Quarterly*, (186), 295–313.

Kipnis, A. (2007). Neoliberalism reified: Suzhi discourse and tropes of neoliberalism in the PRC. *Journal of the Royal Anthropological Institute*, *13*(2), 383–99.

Kipnis, A. (2008). Audit cultures: Neoliberal governmentality, socialist legacy or technologies of governing? *American Ethnologist*, *35*(2), 275–89.

Kipnis, A. (2011). *Governing educational desire: Culture, politics and schooling in China*. Chicago, IL: University of Chicago Press.

LeVine, R. A. & White, M. I. (1986). *Human conditions: The cultural basis of educational development*. Cambridge: Cambridge University Press.

Liu, L., Zhang, R. & Fang, X. (Eds.) (1997). *Ai de wuqu: Zhongxiao xuesheng chengzhang wenti bei wanglu*. Beijing: Zhongguo Renshi Chubanshe.

Ma, Q. (2001). Nongcun suzhi jiaoyu zhi ben shi tigao jiaoshi suzhi. *Suzhou Jiaoyu Xueyuan Xuebao*, (3), 60–1.

Mao, T. (1975). *Selected works of Mao T'se-Tung* (5 vols.). Beijing: Foreign Languages Press.

Murphy, R. (2004). Turning peasants into modern Chinese citizens: 'Population quality' discourse, demographic transition and primary education. *The China Quarterly*, (177): 1–20.

Naftali, O. (2009). Empowering the child: Children's rights, citizenship and the state in contemporary China. *The China Journal* (61), 79–104.

Nie, H. N. (2008). *The dilemma of the moral curriculum in a Chinese secondary school*. Latham, MD: University Press of America.

Ong, A. & Zhang, L. (2008). Introduction: Privatizing China: Powers of the self, socialism from afar. In L. Zhang & A. Ong (Eds.), *Privatizing China: Socialism from afar* (pp. 1–19). Ithaca, NY: Cornell University Press.

Rabinow, P. (1984). Introduction. In P. Rabinow (Ed.), *The Foucault reader* (1st ed., pp. 3–29). New York: Pantheon Books.

Rose, N. (1996). Governing 'advanced' liberal democracies. In A. Barry, T. Osbourne & N. Rose (Eds.), *Foucault and political reason: Liberalism, neo-liberalism, and rationalities of government* (pp. 37–64). Chicago, IL: University of Chicago Press.

Rosen, S. (1989). Value change among post-Mao youth: The evidence from survey data. In E. P. Link, R. Madsen & P. Pickowicz (Eds.), *Unofficial China: Popular culture and thought in the People's*

Republic of China (pp. 193–216). Boulder, CO: Westview.

Rosen, S. (1994). Chinese students in the nineties adjusting to the market. *China News Analysis*, 1–15 August, 1–12.

Shandong Yanjiu Ketizu. (1998). Guanyu ren de suzhi ji qi jiegou de fenxi yu yanjiu. *Shandong Jiaoyu Keyan*, (2), 4–8.

Shore, C. & Wright, S. (2000). Coercive accountability: The rise of audit culture in higher education. In M. Strathern (Ed.), *Audit cultures: Anthropological studies in accountability, ethics, and the academy* (pp. 57–89). London: Routledge.

Sigley, G. (1996). Governing Chinese bodies: The significance of the concept of governmentality for the analysis of government in China. *Economy and Society*, 25(4), 457–82.

Sigley, G. (2004). Liberal despotism: Population planning, subjectivity, and government in contemporary China. *Alternatives*, 24(5), 557–75.

Sigley, G. (2006). Chinese governmentalities: Government, governance and the socialist market economy. *Economy and Society*, 35(4), 487–508.

Stafford, C. (1995). *The roads of Chinese childhood: Learning and identification in Angang*. Cambridge and New York: Cambridge University Press.

Thøgersen, S. (2003). Parasites or civilizers: The legitimacy of the Chinese Communist Party in rural areas. *China: An International Journal*, 1(2), 200–23.

Tomba, L. (2008). Making neighbourhoods: The government of social change in China's cities. *China Perspectives*, (4), 48–61.

Wang, S. (2000). *Please don't call me human* (H. Goldblatt, Trans.) New York: Hyperion East.

Woronov, T. (2003). Transforming the future: 'Quality' children for the Chinese nation. Unpublished PhD thesis, University of Chicago.

Xiaoxue Sixiang Pinde He Zhongxue Sixiang Zhengzhi Jiaocai Bianxie Weiyuanhui (Ed.) (2003). *Sixiang zhengzhi: Er nianji shang*. Beijing: Renmin Jiaoyu Chubanshe.

Xiong, L. & He, C. (2002). Muqian nongcun suzhi jiaoyu cunzai de wenti jiqi duice. *Changsha Daxue Xuebao*, 16(1), 20–2.

Yan, H. (2003). Neoliberal governmentality and neohumanism: Organizing suzhi/value flow through labor recruitment networks. *Cultural Anthropology*, 18(4), 493–523.

Yu, X. (2003). Qiantan guanyu nongcun zhongxiaoxue shishi suzhi jiaoyu de wenti. *Shaanxi Shifan Daxue Jixu Jiaoyu Xuebao (Xian)*, (20), 240–1.

Index

Page numbers in **Bold** represent illustrations.

For Product Safety Concerns and Information please contact our EU
representative GPSR@taylorandfrancis.com
Taylor & Francis Verlag GmbH, Kaufingerstraße 24, 80331 München, Germany